CW00417624

Death
Persuades

by

David McCormac

About the Author

I was born in as small town called Iserlohn, which is in the western part of Germany. I was the second son of Geoffrey and Iris McCormac. Geoffrey was an officer in the British Army and Iris was a wonderful and loving Mother, who passed away almost twenty years ago. After six months of living in Germany, I moved back to England to my mother's home town of Nottingham. After being state educated, I went to a university in London, where I studied History. After three years, I did a P.G.C.E course at Northampton. A year later I moved back to Nottingham, where I have been teaching for the past twenty-five years.

Contents

Monday Morning

Characters

Val Johnson
Val is around five foot ten and is of medium build. She is just coming up to retirement age and now lives alone, as both her disabled daughter and, more recently, her husband have both died. She is the main character in the book.

Celia La-one
Celia is around six foot tall and slim built. Although she is past retirement age, she looks younger due to the makeup and clothes she wears. She is never focused on her work and is always vocal when giving her opinion on something.

Mrs Edwards
A small woman who is nearly eighty years old. She has lived on the estate all her life and has been with her husband for sixty years through thick and thin.

Carol
A woman in her sixties, she is loud and proud and can't wait for the single life again.

Tina
Another woman in her sixties, who through her hard times tries to get all the bargains she can.

Frank
A tall man coming up to retirement. He has worked as a bus driver for over forty years and was a colleague of Val's late husband.

Mrs Irons
A small woman who is in her mid-seventies. She carries on working to fund a weekend away every month. Like many people, she didn't save for a pension.

Vicky and Violet
Two women in their early sixties. Like many on the bus, they have only ever known the estate as home. They are not afraid to

speak their minds.

Tom and Brian

Two young men who share their irritation for women of a certain age.

Setting

Val's front garden

The number sixty four bus

Monday Morning

At around ten o'clock on a freezing cold winters morning, a group of people are standing around a freshly dug grave where the vicar is reading the Lord's Prayer. As the vicar gets to the end of the prayer, one of the mourners collapses to the ground and starts to cry out "Why, Why, Why!" as the coffin is being lowered into the grave. As the mourner lays there, sobbing, she receives a kick from one of the people at the graveside.

At around six o'clock on Monday morning, Val Johnson comes out of her front door in order to catch the 64 bus that will take her to work. As she locks her door and walks down her path, she sees her next door neighbour on her hands and knees digging weeds out of the ground.

Val
Morning Mrs Edwards, whilst you are down there pray for me.

Mrs Edwards
Morning Val, I'm getting too old to be on my knees. *(Slowly, with pain edged on her face, she rises to stand).* Do you know Val, it's been three years that I've been waiting for a knee replacement? It keeps getting cancelled. You pay your National Insurance all your working life and what do you get out of it? Nothing but pain and suffering. I'll tell you what Val, although it goes against all of my principles but, private medical insurance is the way forward. It can save you from a lot of pain and distress and in some cases, extend your life for years. How many people die on waiting lists?

Val
I know what you are saying Mrs Edwards, it's just another thing that makes the dividing line get wider between those who have and those who have not.

Mrs Edwards
As the rich become richer and the poor becomes poorer, I'm sure one day the have nots will say it's time to take to the streets and fight for the terrible injustices that they are having to endure.

Val

We are going a bit deep this morning. Talking of going a bit deep, how come you are on your hands and knees diggings weeds up out of your garden at six in the morning?

Mrs Edwards

Did you not hear the commotion last night?

Val

Well, now you mention it, I did hear something, but I thought it was the sound of my head banging after my fourth glass of red.

Mrs Edwards

It was that no good tosser of a husband of mine.

Val

What's he done this time?

Mrs Edwards

Can you see my eye? *(She moves her face towards the sun)*

Val

Bloody hell. I can now you have moved your head into the light. That's going to be a right shiner, so what happened?

Mrs Edwards

He got in at around one o'clock last night, pissed. I could smell him a mile off. He said he had been down the Dirty Duck pub and they forced him to stay when Ron the landlord had one of his many lock-ins.

Val

The last time the Dirty Duck had a lock in the Mayors wife was standing on the bar with her bra off singing Any Old Iron. The best thing was though she couldn't understand why her, and her husband didn't get re-elected the following year. So, what happened Mrs Edwards?

Mrs Edwards

He tried it on.

Val

He didn't?

Mrs Edwards

He bloody did. He started trying to rip my clothes off, so I told him to piss off and that's when he punched me in the face.

Val
 That's shocking.

Mrs Edwards
 I don't know where I found the strength from, but I pushed him off and ran to the kitchen. I found a rolling pin in the top draw and then ran back into the living room where I found him staggering towards the telly. I hit him over the head three times.

Val
 Why three times?

Mrs Edwards
 Well, I hit him over the head the first time and I said 'that's for giving me a black eye.' The second time I hit him I said 'that's for nicking the house keeping money over the last fifty years,' and the third time, which gave me the most pleasure, I shouted 'and that's for being a crap lover who has never given me any sexual pleasure.'
 (They both laugh)

Val
 We shouldn't laugh.

Mrs Edwards
 It was a good job though when I was hitting him that I didn't remember him going off with my sister as the fourth blow would've killed him.

Val
 Didn't she want to keep him?

Mrs Edwards
You are joking? She took one look at what was between his legs and sent him straight back. If only he was a couple of inches bigger, my sister would've taken him, and my life would've been so much better.

Val
 So, where is he now?

Mrs Edwards
 In hospital. They are saying he will be there for at least a couple of weeks.

Val
 It will give you a break and help your eye heal. But you are not the young, strong willed woman you used to be. There is a good

chance you won't survive the next attack.

Mrs Edwards

I know what you are saying, but I'm eighty this year. I was born and grew up in this area. So to leave a house that I have lived in for the last sixty years and to leave friends and family that I have known all my life would kill me quicker than any drunk could ever do.

Val

But there is a life beyond this estate.

Mrs Edwards

But it is a life that I am just too old to adjust to. Better to die somewhere that you know rather than somewhere that you don't.

Val

But...

Mrs Edwards

Val, we all must go sometime. When my times comes it will be in a house that I know every inch of and an estate that I know like the back of my hand. There is a lot to be said for friendships and familiarity. You are a younger woman Val, with a good personality. Don't stay in a house where all you have is ghosts for company. No-one would think any less of you if life wanted you to discover new adventures. Before I forget the police are coming around later to take my statement.

Val

They don't rush, do they?

Mrs Edwards

It's only a domestic, you know what the police are like when it comes to paperwork. In fairness to them, we want to see the police on the street making us feel safer, rather than stuck behind a desk writing reports that nobody reads.

Val

That's true.

Mrs Edwards

Can I put you down as a witness?

Val

Course you can. Right, I'd better go and catch my bus. I don't want to be late for my shift. See you love.

Mrs Edwards
    See you Val.

*Val starts to walk along Edwards Lane to catch the number 64
bus. Looking at her watch, she quickens her pace as the bus is
due. As she rushes, she see's Carol hanging out her bedroom
window.*

Carol
    Morning Val.

Val
    Morning Carol, how are you love?

Carol
    I'm good love, but that husband of mine has not got too long
left.

Val
    What are we talking, weeks or months?

Carol
    A couple of weeks at the most.

Val
    What are you going to do love?

Carol
    What, when he moves out to be with his slut lover?

Val
    Yes.

Carol
    I'm going to live the life I should have had. I've booked
Benidorm for the middle of July.

Val
    What are you going to do if he's still here?

Carol
    He won't be, believe me. If the two-timing rat has not moved
out by then I'll punch his lights out. *(She holds a glass of wine up)*
Here's to freedom and fun!

Val

Bloody hell Carol, it's a bit early for drinking wine,

Carol

In my new life, wine will be acceptable any time of the day.

Val

See you later love. (They both wave at each other)

Getting to the bus stop, Val sees Tina on her doorstep.

Tina

Val.

Val

Hi Tina.

Tina

Have you still got that offer on eggs?

Val

What, a dozen eggs for two pounds?

Tina

Yes.

Val

It's on till the end of the week.

Tina

And have you still got two for one on toilet rolls?

Val

We have.

Tina

Put them to one side for me, I'll pop in later.

Val

Alright love, leave it with me.

As Tina closes her door, Val see's the bus coming down the road and she gets her purse out. The bus stops and opens the doors.

Frank

Morning Val.

Val

Morning Frank, how are you love?

Frank
I'm good, but more importantly, how are you?

Val
I'm doing alright.

Frank
It must be about six months since you lost him?

Val
It will be six months this Friday.

Frank
He was a fine man your husband, and a bloody good bus driver.

Val
Thank you Frank. *(Val opens her purse)* Frank I've got no change; I paid the window cleaner thinking I had some change in the phone box.

Frank
Don't worry about it, get yourself sat down.

Val
Thanks Frank.

As Val goes to sit down, Mrs Irons shouts over to Val from the back of the bus.

Mrs Irons
Morning Val.

Val
Morning Mrs Irons, you're never still working at your age?

Mrs Irons
I should have retired ten years ago. But that husband of mine keeps telling me that the extra money I bring in allows us to treat ourselves to weekends away.

Val
Well it does get you away. Do you go each month?

Mrs Irons
Usually, but we didn't have the money to go last month on account that the Dog and Bear pub has re-opened after its refurb.

Val
 Do you think you might get away this month?

Mrs Irons
 I doubt it. They have got a two for one offer on spirits now. You wouldn't put a fag out in our bog at the moment, its bound to blow up the whole bloody street. *(Everyone on the bus laughs)*

The bus driver comes up to the next stop and opens the doors.

Frank
 Bloody hell, look at the state of you. Morning Celia, you look like death warmed up.

Celia
 (Getting on the bus) I feel it. (She starts to reach into her pockets looking for change. Vicky and Violet are standing behind Celia looking impatient)

Vicky
 Can you hurry up please it will be nice to get to work sometime this week.

Celia
 Sod off, can't you see I'm not well.

Vicky
 I see it's still two for one down at the Dog.

Celia
 I don't know what you mean.

There are two young men standing behind Vicky and Violet. It is Tom and Brian.

Tom
 Will you hurry up, we were late every day last week because you can never find any change.

Celia
 Piss off, all I've got is a fiver. Val you got any change?

Val
 No, I gave all my change to my window cleaner.

Celia
 Mrs Irons, you got any change?

Mrs Irons
No love I've got a bus pass.

Celia
I'll see if anyone has got any change upstairs. *(She walks up the stairs, five minutes later she comes back down the stairs with a handful of change, but misses the last step, stumbling, dropping it all on the floor)*

Vicky
I don't believe it.

Tom
Bloody hell Grandma, have you always been a nightmare?

Celia
Who you calling a grandma? I'll have you know I eat little boys like you for breakfast.

Frank and Val get on their hands and knees and helps Celia to pick up all her money. After five minutes, Celia pays the bus driver and sits down next to Val. As the other people get on the bus, they all give Celia a filthy look and go and sit down.

Val
I don't know why you don't use your bus pass. It would save you all this hassle.

Celia
Keep your voice down. I don't want anyone knowing my age. It might hinder my chances of getting off with a younger man.

Val
It's time you slowed down a little bit, you are not much used to anyone dead.

Celia
Talking of death, my mouth is as dry as the Savanna Desert and my head will not stop banging.

Val
Here *(opening her bag)* there's two paracetamols and a flask of black coffee.

Celia
You're a star. Open that window I need some fresh air. (Val

opens the window and Violet turns around)

Violet

Excuse me, do you mind shutting that window? It's causing a draft down the back of my legs.

Celia

Yes, I do mind, its being opened for medical reasons and if you are cold you should've put some trousers on instead of a cheap looking dress.

Violet

Cheeky cow. *(Turning to shout at the bus driver)* Bus driver, can you tell this person to shut the window please.

Frank

Excuse me Miss La-One, can you close the window please?

Violet

La-One. *(Her and Vicky start to laugh)* Lets hope La-One doesn't become two, we couldn't be doing with another La-One of her. *(The passengers start to laugh)*

Celia

Well you wouldn't become La-One ever with so much facial hair. Did you forget to shave this morning?

Upon hearing this confrontation, Frank stops the bus and comes out of his cabin.

Frank

If I get anymore arguing I will throw you both off the bus. *(He closes the window)*

Celia

I've opened that window for medical reasons.

Frank

If you open it again your feet will need medical attention when you have to walk to work.

Frank goes back into his drivers cab and starts the bus up. As the bus drives off, Celia's phone begins to ring.

Celia

(In a loud voice) Hello who is this? Graham? Graham who? Graham Peters. *(Turning to Val)* Who is this Graham Peters?

Val
Don't look at me.

Celia
(On the phone) So how come you have got my number? I gave it to you last night in the Dog? I don't think so, what when you brought me my third double vodka? Val, I haven't a clue who this twat is. Wait a minute, are you the guy with the hairy chest and the wondering hands? *(Everyone on the bus applauds and cheers)* Do you mind this is a private conversation. *(Everyone laughs)*

Tom
Private? Not with your gob.

Celia
Graham, I'll have to give you a call back on my lunch break. *(She presses the button to end the call)*

Val
Was he nice?

Celica
He was nice in that he kept putting his hand in his pocket, but as for looks, I can't really remember.

At the back of the bus a young lad puts on his headphones and is listening to some loud music, which can be heard through his headphones.

Brian
Bloody hell, if it's not her gob, it's someone playing loud music.

Celia
(Waving to the young lad who is playing the music). Excuse me. *(The young lad takes off his headphones).* Do you mind not playing that racket so loud? We don't want to hear that noise on a Monday morning. *(Everyone on the bus stares at Celia)*

Val
Right come on this is our stop.

They both get up and walk towards the door. As Celia does, she stops where both Vicky and Violet are sitting.

Celia
Boots sell razors.

As Celia gets off the bus first, she shouts back to Frank 'Thanks!' and blows him a kiss.

Val

You have a good day Frank and give my love to your Maureen.

Frank

You look after yourself.

As the bus drives off, Celia stops and lights up a fag. Val walks ahead, then turns around to Celia.

Val

Come on nightmare or we are going to be late.

The New Recruit

Characters

Sarah Viola

A woman in her early sixties. She is the supervisor of the Happy Convenience. She is very dominant and doesn't like workers who do not pull their weight.

Karen Miller

A medium sized woman in her early thirties. She has had hard times in much of her life due to her upbringing and her choices in men.

Deb

A small woman in her mid-thirties. She is loud an outspoken and doesn't think twice about asking personal questions. She has worked on the deli for years.

Rose

A mother to five and a grandmother to six. She is in her sixties and although very caring, if you get on the wrong side of her then you have a major problem. She looks after Penny.

Penny

A young woman in her mid-twenties. She rarely talks, due to her being raped as a young schoolgirl which has seen her go through a traumatic ten years.

Pam

A woman in her late sixties who, like most of the workers, was born and brought up on the estate, an estate she still lives on. Her belief is if you are alright with me, then I'll be alright with you.

Annie and Joan

Both ladies are of retirement age and have been best friends since primary school. Like many women on the estate they have had their ups and downs but have battled through it together.

Judy

A black woman in her late fifties. She is always friendly and up for a laugh. She works for her holidays and can be found on a Spanish beach at least five times a year. This makes her popular with her work colleagues as she always brings back duty-free goods.

Betty

A small woman in her mid-seventies. She has not had an easy life and is slowing down due to her age and health.

Adam Fletcher

A man in his forties. He is the general manager of the store. Although he does have the workers best interests at heart, he uses his status as the manager to get what he wants personally and professionally.

Setting

In the Happy Convenience Supermarket

The New Recruit

Both Val and Celia stand outside the Happy Convenience Supermarket. As they watch the main doors open and shut, Celia puts her fag out on the pavement.

Val

Who in their right mind calls a supermarket 'The Happy Convenience'?

Celia

I know what you mean. I've never seen a happy customer in here yet.

Val

The staff who work here are only happy when they are shopping in another supermarket.

Celia

Why have we been working here so long?

Val

Because you like to drink and buy clothes.

Celia

And you had to buy the special medicine in order to keep your disabled daughter at home.

Val

Carers never came cheap, especially as they were coming in four times a day, but what could I do when it is your own flesh and blood who was suffering? I knew that she was going to have terrible disabilities when she was inside me, but I couldn't have an abortion when there was a chance, she would have some quality of life. By the age of twenty-one I could see her life was slipping away. As we sang happy birthday to her, her eyes had become dead to the world. Even when we brought in the cake, her mouth showed no signs of a smile, even at the thought of tasting it.

Celia

How long did she last after, what should have been her special day?

Val

Just one day. The next night, the three of us shared the bed and although Ken *(Val's Husband)* couldn't keep his eyes open after a couple of hours, I just kept looking into her eyes, watching them slowly close for the last time. Do you know Celia, when they did close, it was the first time I saw my daughters face at peace in twenty-one years? I told her I loved her very much and knowing that she was ready, I told her to go towards the spiritual light and not to be afraid as mummy's love will be with you wherever your journey takes you.

Celia

(Wiping away a tear) Would you do it all again?

Val

In a heartbeat. Times were tough, but to hold somethings that not only filled you with an amazing love, but to see a smile that lit up the darkest parts of my life was magical. Although my husband and daughter have started their next journey, the memories they have given me has made me feel so blessed that I got to share their life.

Sarah Viola, who is the Happy Convenience Supervisor, known as Viola Vile, comes out of the main doors and shouts to Val and Celia.

Sarah

Is there any chance that you two might want to do some work today?

Celia

I didn't know we were late?

Sarah

That's your problem Miss La-One. You don't know anything when it comes to hard work and commitment, If both of you are not in this store in the next two minutes you can both pick your P45's up from my office. *(Sarah walks back through the doors)*

Celia

I see Viola Vile is just as vile as always. It must have been another weekend she couldn't find a man.

Val

I think we need to give her a helping hand. It might change her attitude and help her to focus on something other than this place. Come on girl, the sooner we start the sooner we finish.

They both walk into the supermarket and head to the locker room, where they both put on their uniforms.

Celia

I don't know who was responsible for the design of these uniforms, but who in their right mind uses the colours blue and green on a uniform?

Val

They always say blue and green should never be seen.

Celia

I'm a person who does need to be seen.

Val

To be seen either propping up a bar or with a man.

Celia

What sort of girl do you think I am?

Val

Slut comes to mind. *(They both laugh)*

Celia

Come on girl before we get the sack.

Both Val and Celia walk through the doors at the back of the supermarket where they are met by Sarah the supervisor.

Sarah

Well it's nice of you two to turn up. Let's see if we can get some work out of you both. Miss La-One, I want you to go on the self-checkouts.

Celia

That's all I need, some mechanical women telling customers to put it in the bagging area or 'someone is coming to help'. It's a shame it's not real or I would slap the bitch.

Sarah

Off you go Miss La-One. *(Celia walks off)* Now as for you Mrs Johnson, I want you to show a new recruit around.

Val

Really?

Sarah

Yes really. Here she comes now. This is Karen Miller, Mrs Johnson is one of our more senior members of staff *(Val glares at Sarah)* who will show you around and introduce you to some of the members of staff. God help you. *(Sarah walks away)*

Val

Don't pay much attention to her, her bark is worse than her bite. Karen isn't it?

Karen

It is.

Val

Well everyone calls me Val. *(As Val says this, one of the employees walks behind walk)*

Employee

Amongst other things.

Val

Sod off. Now as you can see, each aisle has a number above it and a board which lists the items you can buy on that aisle. Now it would be a good idea if you memorised what sort of things are on each aisle. Even if you are put on frozen foods, you will be expected to know where every other product is. The customers get rather ratty if you don't know, especially as everyone is in a rush these days. If you don't know, go with it and bluff it, look as though you do know. Let's go to the main entrance and start at the beginning. *(They both walk outside, then walk through the main doors)* Now on the left you can see all the flowers and plants. Now depending on the time of the week, that will depend on what is dead and what is alive. The flowers that are in buckets of water, always look healthy but the plants in the pots usually don't look so good. Because of health and safety, they are not allowed to be watered. So, hundreds of plants die and are thrown away each month. We must lose thousands of pounds a year. Now straight ahead is the clothing section. Women's and children's clothes at the front, men's at the back. The women spend more, hence why their clothes are in the front. At the side of the clothing section was the changing rooms but management closed them, wanting the customers to take the purchase home to try on. You might be thinking is this the best strategy?

Karen

I was.

Val

Think, how many people forget to bring the item back or lose their receipt? A guaranteed profit. As you can see there are twelve aisles, separated into two halves. Now I believe Miss Viola wants you to spend this afternoon going down each aisle memorising each item that is on that aisle, good luck with that, but don't forget management will test you on what items are on what aisle at the end of the week. So, what we will do now is to take you to meet some of the strange and interesting people that work here. *(Val lifts her eyes. They walk to the deli bar)* Now this is Deb's domain, or as she is known, ' Dozen Deb.' Don't ask, but she doesn't have a great figure like that by dieting. Morning Deb.

Deb

Morning Val, how are you doing?

Val

I'm good thanks. This is Karen, it's her first day.

Deb

Hello love, are you single?

Val

Don't beat around the bush, after all it is your first-time meeting.

Karen

Yes, I am, my last boyfriend cheated on me.

Deb

Did he cheat on you with a younger woman who couldn't say no?

Karen

No, he cheated on me with an older man who was very well endowed.

Deb

Well it's his loss. By the sounds of it you need to party more. You will have to come out with me one night. I get invited to all the best parties.

Karen

Thanks, I will let you know. *(Val and Karen walk away)*

Val

The parties she is referring to are more underwear than evening gowns.

Karen

Really?

Val

Really.

Val and Karen walk down the first aisle, which is the frozen section. Working on this aisle is Penny and Rose.

Rose

Morning Val.

Val

Morning Rose. I'm just showing our new recruit around. Karen, meet Rose and Penny.

Karen

Hello, it is nice to meet you both. Have you been here long?

Rose

Too bloody long. I wanted to leave ten years ago, but when you have got five kids that have grown up to think safe sex are two words that shouldn't be spoken, that's why I'm a granny to six. With birthdays, and Christmas presents to buy, you can see why I'm still here.

Val

Well with five kids, condoms was a word you didn't speak about. *(They all laugh)*

Rose

That's what you get when you live next door to a pub.

Val

Right come on Karen, let's leave them both to the mercy of the frozen veg.

Rose

See you Val.

Val

See you girls. (They walk off)

Karen

They seem nice.

Val

They are in their own way. Although, keep on Rose's good side. She can be a nasty bitch if you cross her. Half of our taxes have been spent on keeping her five kids at Her Majesties pleasure. As for Penny,

Karen

She didn't talk.

Val

She won't. It's very rare that she says anything.

Karen

Why is that?

Val

She was walking home from school one day when she was jumped by two young men. They dragged her, kicking and screaming into the bushes and raped her repeatedly for over an hour. When they had finished, they left her bleeding and traumatised. It took her two hours to stumble home, a journey that usually takes two minutes. When she got home, her screaming mother phoned for an ambulance. When she got to the hospital, they rushed her into the operating theatre, she had lost a lot of blood.

Karen

Did the police find who did this?

Val

They did, but Penny's father found them first, and as an ex-boxer, he beat them both to a pulp and the knife he took with him was used to remove various organs. Because of that one hour, two young rapists had mentally seen their lives end. A father has lost ten years of his life in a maximum-security unit, and a young fifteen-year-old girl was left without speech and suffering an intense depression. She turned into herself for comfort. Although with the help of doctors and psychiatrists, she started to bring herself out of that dark place.

Karen

There is always someone worse off than yourself.

Val

Isn't that the truth.

They both walk to aisle five, the tins section.

Pam

Morning Val.

Val

Morning Pam, no Paula today?

Pam

No, she's called in sick.

Val

What is it this time?

Pam

An anxiety attack.

Val

Was that brought on because she thought she might have to do a full day's work?

Pam

Something like that, although she is up before the disciplinary committee next week. They have been asking if anyone would like to speak in her defence.

Val

Is there anyone?

Pam

Not one. Although it's not the best place to work, with long hours and low pay, but she does take the piss.

Val

Let's hope she will piss off. *(They both laugh)* By the way, this is Karen, our new recruit.

Karen

Hello.

Pam

Hiya love. Welcome to the Happy Convenience. Let's hope you

enjoy being here as much as we do.

Val
Alright Pam love, don't over do it. Your job doesn't involve being a PR Agent.

Pam
Well it is her first day.

Val
And if you carry on it'll be your last day. *(They both laugh)* I'll see you later Pam.

Both Val and Karen walk to aisle thirteen.

Karen
Aisle thirteen.

Val
Lucky for some, but then unlucky for others.

Karen
Why's that?

Val
Well, lucky because you don't have to go to the offie to get a bottle or two, you can get it here with your discount card, but unlucky when you are fuelling a relative's habit which has blighted many a family. Talking about drinking too much, this is Annie and Joan, our two resident alcoholics.

Annie
Don't listen to her love, there's only one alcoholic in here and that's mine's a double, our pal Val.

Val
Cheeky cow. Ladies this is our new recruit, Karen.

Joan
Hello love and welcome to the zoo.

Val
If you need any advice about wines and spirits, then Joan is your girl, since she has tried them all, more than once.

Joan
If you don't try you'll never know.

Annie

That's true enough.

Joan

Do you remember Val when we went out on that works do and we went to the Rose and Crown for last orders?

Val

Do I ever.

Annie

Trouble was though, it wasn't the last one of the night, it was the first of many.

Karen

Why was that?

Joan

Well we were all sitting at the bar when the landlord started to slur his words and pointing to his heart. Well we all thought that he was drinking his profits away, hence the reason when he collapsed on the floor, we just thought he was pissed, so we continued drinking.

Val

And drinking. These two thought they would be barmaids for the night, stepping over the landlord, they both started serving drinks free of charge. Well at four o'clock in the morning with everyone drunk, alcoholics anonymous over there noticed that the landlord was turning a dark shade of blue.

Joan

He wasn't looking good.

Val

I'm not surprised, he was bloody dead.

Annie

He was and to think as he was dying, they were playing 'I will survive' on the karaoke machine.

Val

What time did you ring for an ambulance?

Joan

Six o'clock, there were two full bottles of gin to get through.

Annie
Well at least we gave him a good send off.

Joan
I heard the tight git didn't even have a wake.

Val
Right Karen, let me take you away from these two piss heads. See you later ladies.

Annie/Joan
See you later Val.

They both walk to the checkouts.

Val
Now this is called checkout alley. There are ten self-check outs and ten manual checkouts, although you will be lucky to see more than four manual ones open at any one time.

Karen
Why is that?

Val
Because the boss man won't employ enough workers to run his supermarket. Now at checkout number one we have got the wonderful Judy, who as you can see is looking amazing since she is never off a beach in or around Spain.

Judy
(Shouting from her till) Hello Val.

Val
Alright Judy love? When you flying?

Judy
Next Tuesday. I've got to stock up on my fags and booze and my tan of course.

Val
Isn't it your big birthday this year?

Judy
Yeah, my fifth.

Val
Of course it is.

Judy

It's all round to mine next month.

Val

I'll book the week off.

Judy

Make sure you do.

Val

(To Karen) Your head is still banging three days after the event.

Karen

Why is that?

Val

Something to do with the fact that she has got every alcoholic beverage known to man. Now on checkout number two we have the amazing Betty who doesn't know what it's like to get a sweat on. Customers have been known to bring their sleeping bags with them due to the time they have to wait to get served. Although, due to her poor eyesight and arthritis they are lucky to get served at all.

Karen

Why has she carried on after retirement age?

Val

Like a lot of people, they never put into a pension pot. When you are in your twenties you never think you will become a pensioner, so many people think of the moment and not for the future.

Betty

Alright Val.

Val

I'm fine Betty love. You take it east now.

Betty

I'm trying to, but as you can see, I've got a queue a mile long. I don't know why they don't go to any of the other checkouts. They've hardly got any customers.

Val

(To Karen) Maybe because they do their jobs much quicker. Now at checkout number three we have the lovely Sheila.

Sheila

Hi Val, you well?

Val

I'm good.

Karen

She seems nice?

Val

Usually she is, but it all depends on what costume she is wearing.

Karen

What do you mean?

Val

Well her and her husband like to dress up.

Karen

Really?

Val

Yes. A few years ago, they went out on a Saturday night dressed as Laurel and Hardy. When they got home, the bedroom saw a lot of action and a few weeks later Sheila told her husband she was pregnant. Do you now what her husband said?

Karen

What?

Val

"Here's another fine mess you have got into Stanley" *(they both laugh)* The best one was when they conceived their second child.

Karen

Why?

Val

They were dressed as Batman and Robin. When she told her husband he said, "Let's go to the Batmobile to celebrate."

Karen

No.

Val

They put on the Batman music in the car and drove around in

their Batman and Robin outfits.

Karen

What can I say?

Val

Say nothing, that way you don't fall out with anyone. Finally, on the self-checkout we have got Miss La-One.

Karen

What's her last name?

Val

La-One, she changed it by deed pole, but it was Butcher, but she thought it wouldn't attract the right type of men.

Karen

What type is that?

Val

The rich, well-educated ones.

Karen

It seems pretty empty at the self-checkouts.

Val

Her abrupt, don't mess with me attitude doesn't always go down well with the customers. Last week a customer kept getting their things wrong, which of course gets the machine talking to you. After ten minutes of the machine saying 'an assistant is coming to help you' Celia slapped the machine and told the customer to go to another checkout. She said she couldn't stand to hear that bitch on the machine's voice anymore.

Karen

Had she been out the night before?

Val

Every night before.

Celia

(Shouting) Val love the manager wants to see us.

Val

(Shouting back) Okay.

Celia

I'll just get Pat known as Paul to take me off.

Karen

(Walking back towards the back of the store) Who is Pat known as Paul?

Val

Pat is transitioning into Paul. A while back Paul was telling me that for years that he felt something wasn't right as he couldn't identify with his body as Pat. Men came and went because the role as Pat she was expected to play, never felt right in all aspects of her life. So, he took a leap of faith and decided to get the body he was happy with. The breasts went a couple of months ago and the penis is arriving next month. As you will see, his body hair is like a national forest, a bit different as Pat where he was going for a wax every week. He said he saves loads of money.

Karen

There comes a time you must live life for you and not for other people.

Val

Well said. Right, I'll see you later.

Val heads to the managers office, as she does, Celia catches up with her.

Celia

You don't think he is going to sack us, do you?

Val

Some hope of that, unless he has finally found out about your made-up story of having a water infection so that you can go to the toilet via the fag shelter.

Celia

I can't help it if things are not right down below.

Val

Is it four or five years you have had this problem?

Celia

It's resilient, I must admit.

Val

And every time you go to the chemist, they're shut.

Celia

They are not very reliable.

Val

At least the pubs are more reliable for you.

Celia

How rude!

Val

You mean how rude it would be of him to turn an offer of a drink down.

Val

Never. *(Sarcastically)*

Celia

That's alright then.

Val knocks on Adam Fletcher's door. He is the manager of the Happy Convenience.

Adam

Come in.

Val

(They both walk in) Did you want to see us?

Adam

I do ladies. *(Both Val and Celia stand alongside the manager's desk)* I want you both to do me a big favour.

Celia

Of course, we will.

Adam

As you both know, Mrs Greensmith passed away a couple of weeks ago. Now I know she wasn't the most popular member of staff due to her nasty attitude with anyone that came near her, but she was part of the Happy Convenience family for over twenty years and because of that, we should send someone to represent us at the funeral.

Val

How does that involve us?

Adam

It is you two I have chosen to represent us.

Val

Do you think that's a good idea?

Adam

I do.

Celia

But the only time we ever communicated with her is when we argued with her.

Adam

At least you were communicating with her, that's more than most people ever did. Now I have checked the rota and you are both off that day so I'm sure you don't want to let me or the Happy Convenience down.

Val

(In a low voice) No, of course not.

Adam

Thank you ladies for helping us out.

Celia

You're welcome.

Val and Celia turn around and walk out of the room.

Val

That's all I bloody need.

Revelations

Characters

Simon
An overweight solicitor who is in his sixties.

Vicar
A tall man in his fifties.

Samantha
A small woman in her late twenties. She is the daughter of Liz Greensmith. From leaving school she has been mixed up in drugs and drink and would think nothing of robbing her mother to fund her habits.

Michael
A tall man in his early twenties. He is the boyfriend of Samantha and shares some of her habits.

Setting
In and outside of the Church.

Revelations

On a warm and sunny morning, Val and Celia stand outside the Church, waiting for the funeral procession to arrive.

Celia

Well, this is a nice way to start our day off.

Val

You're right, I've got a stack of ironing to do and I'm sure the weeds are looking to take over the garden.

Celia

I have a man who can do all those sorts of jobs.

Val

Are we still talking about weeds? *(They both laugh)*

Celia

Well, I hope the Vicar doesn't want me to talk about her as all I could say to the mourners is that she was an angry, argumentative woman who spent her time sitting on her own reading books.

Val

She left one of her books in the canteen area.

Celia

Did she? What was it called?

Val

Humanitarian Aid Around the World.

Celia

She never seemed to be the caring type.

Val

There are two sides to everybody.

Celia

Did she have any family?

Val

I think she had a daughter who on all accounts turned out to be a nasty piece of work who would scrounge every penny from her mother's purse that she could. I believe in the end; her mother offered her five thousand pounds if she would never cross her doorstep again.

Celia

Did she take the money?

Val

She did. But a year later she came knocking on her mother's door.

Celia

Did she let her in?

Val

No, and from that day she never saw her daughter again.

Celia

I don't think I could be that harsh.

Val

She wouldn't be the first who had run out of patience.

Celia

What do you mean?

Val

Think of all these sons and daughters who take drugs. Robbing their mothers of their hard-earned cash and their dignity every time they allow them to walk through their front doors and when they do, what piece of jewellery have they stolen to feed their habit, or which neighbour doesn't communicate with you anymore, even though you have been friends for over twenty years. There comes a time when you must stop helping as it's doing more harm than good, even though your heart is breaking.

Celia

There's someone walking up the Church path.

Val

We won't be the only ones in the congregation.

Two ladies walk up the path and into the Church, they nod as they pass Celia and Val.

Celia

Is red shoes and yellow trousers really the right thing to wear at a funeral?

Two more people walk up the path, a man and a woman.

Val
Good morning.

Lady
Good morning. It's a nice day for it.

Val
As nice as it could be for a funeral.

Lady
Were you friends of Liz?

Val
We were work colleagues. What about yourself?

Lady
Liz was our aunt, but we hadn't seen her for years.

Val
Why was that?

Lady
There was a family feud and she cut herself off from everyone.
See you later. *(They both walk into the Church)*

Celia
It's like an Agatha Christie novel. Here comes another
mourner.

A man walks up the path carrying a briefcase.

Simon
Good morning, ladies.

Val/Celia
Good morning.

Simon
One of you wouldn't be Mrs Johnson by any chance?

Val
Yes, that's me.

Simon
I have an envelope for you that the late Mrs Greensmith wanted
you to read at the funeral.

Val

Really? But I hardly knew her.

Simon

These are my instructions from the late Mrs Greensmith. *(He passes the envelope to Val)* Right I've got to go.

Celia

Are you not coming in?

Simon

No, I have a nearby divorce to sort out. The wife is demanding half of her husband's fortune.

Celia

How large?

Simon

Twenty million.

Celia

Bloody hell, give me his address and I'll pop round to hold his hand.

Simon

Well of course, I can't reveal these sorts of details, but it is someone you know.

Celia

Who is it?

Simon

Bye ladies. *(He walks off)*

Celia

Val, what could we do with that amount of money?

Val

We are at a funeral you know.

Celia

But we are still in the land of the living.

Val

Right come on let's get in, a seat at the back would be best.

Both Val and Celia walk into the Church and sit at the back.

Celia

There's a few more than we thought I see.

Val

Do you know it is six months today that we were sitting in this Church, all be it, I was at the front.

Celia

Is it really six months since that lovely husband of your passed away?

Val

It is, it was a cold and nasty day in more ways than one.

Celia

It certainly was. Are you getting better mentally in coping with your loss?

Val

If you mean am I sleeping better and not waking up in the middle of the night imagining he is lying there next to me, then I am getting better as I mostly sleep through now without waking up once. But when it comes to thinking about him every hour of the day, then that's where I am still suffering. It wouldn't be so bad if I knew where he died and what it was that brought his heart attack on.

Celia

Let's hope you find out one day. All I know is he was very special and a great friend to me.

Val

That's nice to hear. Although you didn't have to collapse on the graveside looking as though you were in one of your stage productions.

Celia

Well, you didn't have to kick me.

Val

Seeing as it was my husband that died, I did.

Celia

It wasn't just about you, there were other people in his life.

Val

That as it maybe, but none as important as his wife. Right, now shut up, here comes the coffin.

As everyone stands up in the congregation, four pallbearers carry in the coffin. Behind the coffin is the deceased's daughter and her younger boyfriend. They are both smiling as they walk down the aisle.

Celia

Look at them smiling and laughing.

Val

It's obvious that they have no feelings or respect for the dead.

The coffin is placed onto the table and the Vicar walks up the steps to the pulpit.

Vicar

Welcome everyone. Now, although the passing of Elizabeth Greensmith is a very sad thing to have happened, it does however allow us to celebrate a brave and remarkable lady.

Celia

(To Val) What's he on about?

Vicar

Elizabeth, or Liz as she was known, was a person who after leaving school went to train at the Royal College of Nursing where she graduated after three years with a first-class degree. Now in most cases, nurses who had qualified went into hospitals to work on the wards, but in Elizabeth's case she went to work as a nurse overseas where she found herself tending to the sick and the dying in war torn areas, often under gunfire. Elizabeth also found herself in countries that were prone to famine, where trying to save the undernourished children became an uphill battle. On one occasion, Elizabeth found herself being the only person with any medical experience in an area that had a population of around five thousand people. With a small medical centre that Elizabeth had set up, there was a small wall that circled the centre. Each day Elizabeth Greensmith would have to decide which starving child would be allowed inside of the wall and who would have to stay on the outside of the wall. Although there was a desperate shortage of food on the inside of the wall, the people were able to have a meal a day that kept them alive. Whereas on the outside of the wall gave Elizabeth a view of death daily. It must have been hell for Elizabeth to have seen so much pain and death and not be able to do anything about it. After a few months, with her health starting to decline due to the fact that she would give most of her food away in order to help save the lives of these who had nothing, Elizabeth, who had lost over half of her body weight, found herself back in England, but with the horrors she had seen and the anger that had built up inside of her, she felt she couldn't carry on as a nurse and left the profession.

Celia
Well, you could knock me down with a feather.

Val
(Wiping away a tear) Having gone through all that, no wonder she was like she was.

Vicar
After leaving the nursing profession, she worked at various places before settling at the Happy Convenience Supermarket. While working there, she met and married her husband Darren, and they had a daughter together, Samantha, who is sitting with us today. We send our deepest condolences for the loss of your mother.

Samantha
(Smiling) Don't worry about it, I'm not. *(Gasps can be heard coming from the mourners)*

Vicar
Now, we have a reading from Mrs Valerie Johnson.

Val stands up and walks to the front of the Church, where she takes an envelope out of her bag.

Val
Good morning everyone. Half an hour ago I was given an envelope to read out to you all today. But before I do, I would just like to say what an amazingly brave woman Liz Greensmith was and what Liz had to go through now has given us all a better understanding of why Liz enjoyed a more solitary existence.

Samantha
Come on love, we all have better places to be.

Michael
The pubs have just opened. Sammy's got enough money now to buy all of you a drink.

Val

(*Opening up the envelope, she reads the letter to the mourners*) If you are reading this letter now, it must mean my end has finally come. Although I have seen and heard things that no one should ever see in their lives, there were parts of my life that I found enjoyable, although grief was never far away in reality and my mind. Now you might have been wondering Val, why have I given you the job of reading my last wishes? Well, as I was just starting out as a nurse, I met a wonderful doctor who in just a short time I fell head over heels in love with. Now although he was married and had his own family, I couldn't stop myself from giving him my whole self. After being together for three months, I was sent to the famine areas of Africa. While working there, I found out I was pregnant. I couldn't have an abortion, but If I was to keep my baby, it would take me away from saving lives as I would have had to have time off so many around me didn't have. So I gave my baby to a missionary couple, named John and Alison. They were both from London and promised to look after her, bringing my daughter up as their own. Because you lost your daughter Val, you know and understand the pain that I felt. Talking of daughters, to my waste of space daughter Samantha, who is just as rotten as her father, I leave nothing. But to my beautiful baby girl, who I named Poppy, I leave her everything that is mine to give. (*Samantha and her boyfriend storm out of the Church*) Val, I have left you some details, although somewhat sketchy, I hope you will be able to find her and if you do, tell her I love her so much and hope she can forgive me one day. (*Val looks towards the mourners*) Let's hope I can find her.

Vicar

(*As Val walks back to her seat*) God be with you on your journey, Mrs Johnson.

I'm Getting There

Characters

Lillian
A well-meaning woman in her seventies. Like many of the women in her community, she rarely ventures out of what they know and understand.

Molly
Very much like Lillian, Molly is the same and has the same understanding when it comes to the community that she lives in. Although Molly likes to voice her opinion, but never walks the walk.

Mrs Riley
Her and her husband are in their nineties, with Ken (her husband) dying with Alzheimer's. Having been married for nearly seventy years, death would not keep them apart.

Bev
A woman in her mid-fifties and loves to have a gossip. Gossip that she will act upon if it is to her advantage.

Shelley
A slim sized woman in her mid-fifties. She is the checkout supervisor who is caring enough to give anyone a helping hand. She expects the people around her to work hard and be as loyal as she is.

Mrs Spears
A woman in her seventies and, like many women of her age, has always wanted to stay living in an area that she knows, even if her life has become poorer by staying in a place she knows.

Ricky
A gay man in his mid-thirties, he believes that the men who come into his life should put him first and everything else second. He has been a single man for most of his life.

Jenny
A young woman in her mid-twenties. Jenny has found that life can be very cruel. She has always attracted bad men who have used and abused her, as a result she has been left with four

children and no money to bring up her family.

Setting

Val's back garden

The Happy Convenience Supermarket

I'm Getting There

Two weeks later Val is seen hanging out her washing in her back garden. As she does, she hears someone calling her.

Lillian

Val, are you there?

Val

(Val stands on a wooden crate and looks over her garden wall) Hello Lillian love, how are you?

Lillian

I'm well thanks. Now don't keep me in suspense, are you getting any closer to finding Liz's lost child?

Val

Well, I've contacted the Catholic Church's and explained the situation, they are going to get back to me. I've also been to the registry office to see if any babies had been registered of a daughter called Poppy, and I gave them the date she was born, I said I was sorry there wasn't much to go on, but they did say they would do their best to find her.

Lillian

Well, it's a start, and you never know what might come out of it.

Val

Fingers crossed.

Lillian

Looking at Mrs Edwards back garden, I think she has given up.

Val

It does seem the weeds are winning the war.

Lillian

To think she once had the best back garden for miles around.

Val

Am afraid age and that husband she married have seen the decline when it comes to her garden.

Molly

(Next door but two) Why is it that a seventy-year-old woman down the road is still allowed to rent a three-bedroom council

house when there are hundreds of people with families on the waiting list?

Lillian

Well, I did hear that she offered to move if the council got her a one-bedroom bungalow, but you know the council.

Val

We do know the council, when bins are not emptied, and potholes are not filled. The days when they gave the street a bit of sand to put on the snow are long gone.

Molly

But days when they froze the council tax increases is another thing, that is long gone as well.

Lillian

I'm paying over a hundred quid a month just to have my bins emptied. What's that all about?

Molly

And I'll tell you something else.

Val

Here we go.

Molly

Why is it her at number 86 has her music blaring out all hours of the day and night?

Lillian

I know what you mean.

Molly

It wouldn't be so bad, but all she listens to is heavy metal music.

Val

Well, she was a rock chick in her day.

Molly

You would think at nearly ninety though she would have grown out of it.

Val

I would love to gossip longer but I'm on the afternoon shift, so I must get myself ready.

Molly
I don't know how you have lasted there so long.

Val
Bills love, they need paying. See you all later.

Half an hour later, Val appears at her front door. As she locks the door and walks through her front gate she stares back at her house and says to herself "The time is coming" and walks down the road. Mrs Riley is standing at her front door.

Mrs Riley
Hello Val.

Val
Hello Mrs Riley, you alright?

Mrs Riley
Yes thanks Val, you couldn't get me a few bits? I've wrote them down.

Val
Of course I can. *(Val takes the shopping list)* I'll pop in after work.

Mrs Riley
Thank you love.

Val continues walking along the road towards the bus stop.

Bev
(Standing at her gate) You alright Val?

Val
I'm good.

Bev
Have you heard?

Val
Heard what?

Bev
Carol at number 22, she's had a breakdown.

Val
What's brought that on?

Bev

Well, you know how that two-timing rat of a husband of hers, who she couldn't wait to get rid of?

Val

Yes.

Bev

Well, I heard, and you know I'm not one to gossip.

Val

Of course you are not Bev.

Bev

But just as he was leaving, she had a phone call from the bank manager telling her that that the mortgage hadn't been paid for six months and they were going to repossess the house.

Val

No.

Bev

When she confronted him as he was just about to walk out of the door for the last time, he turned around and gave her a bunch of red letters and said,"Have a good life, I know I will."

Val

That's shocking. Didn't she know how much debt she was in?

Bev

She hadn't got a clue. He took charge of all the financial stuff. They were up to their eyeballs in debt. Nothing had been paid for months. She went round to the new lover's place, but all she got was a bucket of water thrown down over her from the bathroom. Although the water didn't look very clean.

Val

That doesn't bare thinking about, where is she going to go?

Bev

Back to her mother's?

Val

Is she still alive?

Bev

She is, strong as an ox that one, but they have never got on for years and so haven't spoken to each other for a very long time.

Val

That's going to be hell for her. Just when you think you're on the up, life kicks you down again. Well at least she has her holiday to look forwards to.

Bev

She would have done if she had any spending money to go with, which is sad as she has paid for her flight and accommodation.

Val

That is a shame, to see a good holiday go to waste.

Bev

That's what I though, so I went round and offered her a couple of hundred pounds to go in her place.

Val

Did you?

Bev

I did. She moaned that the holiday had cost her a couple of thousands, five-star luxury Val, but what could she do.

Val

What could she?

Bev

Her loss was my gain. I'm really looking forward to it.

Val

I shouldn't send her a postcard.

Bev

I won't have time; I'll be enjoying myself too much.

Val

There's my bus coming.

Bev

See you Val.

As Val runs for the bus, she says to herself "What goes around comes around." After spending twenty minutes on the bus, Val walks into the Happy Convenience, where she is met by Karen who has now been working at the Happy Convenience for the last four weeks.

Karen
Have you heard?

Val
Heard what?

Karen
Celia has been suspended.

Val
What's she done this time?

Karen
Well, she was working alongside Smelly Fred. Which didn't put her in a good mood to start with when a customer complained.

Val
What about?

Karen
An out-of-date label on a tin of peas.

Val
It happens.

Karen
It does, but Celia was on tins yesterday and should have checked all of the out of date stock and removed it.

Val
But of course, Celia being Celia had other things on her mind, how did she sort out the complaint?

Karen
She threw the tin of peas at the customer. It marked her face.

Val
Bloody hell. There will be no coming back from this.

Sarah Viola comes towards Val and Karen.

Sarah
Have you got no work to do Miss Miller?

Karen
I'm just heading to frozen.

Sarah

The speed you get there will warm you up. *(Karen rushes off)* Now Mrs Johnson, as you have no doubt heard, Miss La-One has really done it now.

Val

Has she got any chance?

Sarah

Let's just say, she needs a miracle to survive.

Val

Who's representing her at the tribunal?

Sarah

Now, there's a problem.

Val

Why, isn't Fred the union rep?

Sarah

He is, but this is Celia La-One we are talking about, and as Celia and Fred have never, let's say, hit it off.

Val

True

Sarah

That is why I have put your name down to represent her.

Val

Are you having a laugh?

Sarah

I wish I was, but due to the severity of the offence that was carried out, there's only you that likes her enough to have any chance of saving her. You're on checkout number two, Judith is on the plane as we speak.

Val walks to the checkout alley, where she is met by Shelly, the checkout supervisor.

Shelley

You alright Val?

Val

I was up to two minutes ago.

Shelley

What's happened?

Val

Well, you heard about Celia?

Shelley

The tin throwing maniac.

Val

That's her. Well, they have told me I'm the one they have put down to represent her.

Shelley

Bloody hell. You would have more chance winning the lottery than getting Miss La-One off the hook.

Val

And don't I know it.

Shelley

Right, I've opened number two's checkout for you. Any problems give us a shout.

Val

Will do.

Val settles herself in, and after five minutes staring at a young man trying to decide which flowers to buy, Mrs Spears comes over to Val with her shopping.

Mrs Spears

Are you open love?

Val

Hello Mrs Spears, I'm open as a book.

Mrs Spears

I hope it's a good book.

Val

Bestseller of course.

Mrs Spears

I'm reading a book at the moment.

Val

What's it called?

Mrs Spears
'The Estate'.

Val
Who's it by?

Mrs Spears
No idea, but it's true to life and you feel you know the people in the book. I'll give it to you when I've finished it.

Val
Thanks. Give us your bags and I'll pack them for you.

Mrs Spears
You are kind.

Val
(Whilst packing the bags) How are these grandchildren of yours?

Mrs Spears
Lucy is doing ever so well at school and all the teachers like her. But Daniel is a little sod who is always getting into trouble. He said to one of the teachers the other day "Miss, I'm finding it hard keeping up with these girlfriends." The teacher said, "Why don't you just have one?" and he replied with "But I wouldn't have as many presents for my birthday."

Val
How old is he?

Mrs Spears
Five. *(They both laugh)* How are you, Val?

Val
I keep battling on.

Mrs Spears
I've known you for many years and I know what happened to you was shocking, but there is something troubling you which is preventing you from finding that happiness that you deserve.

Val
I've come to a crossroads, and I just don't know which road to take.

Mrs Spears
Well, you know if you stay on the same road, it's more of the same, but turn to another road and you could be smiling every day.

Val
But I was born here, I know the people around me.

Mrs Spears
You also know you are not happy. Do you really want to spend the rest of your life doing the same old things day in day out?

Val
What if everything goes wrong?

Mrs Spears
What if everything goes right and you are the happiest woman on the planet? Take a leap of faith my girl. Right, how much do I owe you?

Val
Twenty-five pounds ninety.

Mrs Spears
My mother would have said "How much, I've got nothing to show for it."

Val
My mother would have said the same thing.

Mrs Spears
See you next week love.

Val
Bye love. Be careful how you go.

Next to come to Val's checkout is Ricky.

Ricky
Do you know when I first joined the queue for your till I had a full head of hair, now look at me. *(Ricky's hair is very thin on top)*

Val
Hello Ricky, is your grumpy attitude down to being dumped again?

Ricky
I don't know why I bother with men, they're only after one

thing really.

Val

Really?

Ricky

Really. Those first few days we talked about living together, going on holidays and out for meals, theatre, you name it. But as soon as I let them in my bed, the next morning they leave and that's the last I hear from them.

Val

But you do tend to go for married men.

Ricky

I always tell them I don't mind visiting their kids but don't bring them near me. See you love.

Val

Bye Ricky. *(To herself)* and he wonders why he never sees them again.

Jenny is the next person to come to Val's till.

Jenny

Hello Val.

Val

Hello Jenny, I've not seen you in here for a bit, where's the children?

Jenny

They're at school. I'm going to pick them up when I'm done here.

Val

How you coping love? Having four kids under ten can't be easy?

Jenny

I'm trying my best, but I can't keep running up the down escalator every bloody day. *(Tears start to fall down Jenny's cheeks)* I get barely enough to live on each week. Their fathers give me nothing even though they are down the pub each night or going on holidays two or three times a year. They don't see their children's faces when they get nothing for their birthdays or Christmas and although they tell me the only present they need is having us all together, but I can see in their faces they just want to be like every other child who looks forwards to seeing what Santa has brought them. The reason you haven't seen me in here is because most weeks you will find me queuing outside the doors waiting for handouts. Every week I have to stand there with people walking past me thinking I'm dirt and so below them. The food they give me doesn't last half the week, never mind the whole week.

Val

Hence the reason why you have lost weight.

Jenny

I'm not letting the children go hungry.

Val

Don't you ever forget you are as good as anyone else. In fact, better. Who would give up the basics for themselves to see their children not go without. Right my girl, you have got ten minutes to fill that trolley starting from now.

Jenny

But...

Val

Now!

Jenny can be seen racing around the supermarket filling up her trolley. Ten minutes later, Jenny is back at Val's checkout with a full trolley. The price of the items light up.

Jenny

I haven't got three hundred pounds.

Val

(Pressing a button, the amount is deleted) Thank you very much madam (and handing her a twenty pounds note from her pocket) and here is your change.

Jenny

(Holding both of Val's hands, and with tears rolling down her face) Thank you.

Val

Be off with you and go and pick up the kids.

Jenny

Thank you. *(Jenny walks slowly to the door, pushing a full trolley)*

Val

Shelley love it's time I wasn't here.

Shelley

Hold on, I'll just get Sheila to take you off. *(Shouting)* Sheila, are you ready?

Sheila

I'm on my way!

Sheila walks down number tens aisle to the checkout alley. She is walking flat footed towards Val and Shelley.

Val

Bloody hell Sheila have you done yourself an injury?

Sheila

No, I went out last night to a fancy-dress party. I went as Charlie Chaplain. My knees seem to have locked themselves to one side.

Shelley

It's a good job you were not dressed as a crab. *(They all laugh)*

Val

See you both later.

Val walks off in the direction of the lockers. Half an hour later, she is knocking on Celia's door.

Celia

Go away, I'm dying.

Val

If you don't open this door now you won't be dying, you'll be dead. *(Val bangs on the door again)*

Celia

(Opening the door) Do you have to make so much noise? I'm feeling rather delicate.

Val

(Pushing herself through the door) What, as delicate as that woman was when you threw a tin of peas at her head?

Celia

Don't remind me, I don't know what came over me.

Val

I know what came over you, too much alcohol and a bad attitude.

Celia

What are you trying to say?

Val

I'm saying it's time you sorted yourself out.

Celia

What do you mean?

Val

Firstly, your daily trips to the boozer has got to stop. Once or twice a week is enough for any woman in her sixties.

Celia

I'm fifty-nine, and I only go to one pub.

Val

You only go to one pub because every other pub around here has barred you. As for being fifty-nine, you'd better send your bus pass back.

Celia

How dare you. They sent that by mistake.

Val

And is it a mistake that when customers ask for your help you reply, "Don't you think you're old enough to help yourself?" or "I've got better things to do with my time than take you to find something that is less than a fiver?"

Celia

I wouldn't say that.

Val

You say it at least five times a day. How you have still got a job I'll never know. But now you are throwing tins at customers, you have moved up to another level.

Celia

What am I going to do?

Val

As they want me to represent you at the tribunal, you will sit there and say nothing until I nudge you to speak. I hope you are as good on the stage as you say you are because you will need to give the performance of your life. Let's hope it's not the final curtain. Right, I'll see you in the morning.

Walking out of Celia's house with a carrier bag in hand, Val walks down the road and five minutes later is knocking on Mrs Riley's door. Mrs Riley opens her door.

Mrs Riley

Hello Val, you made it.

Val

Sorry Mrs Riley, I should have been here an hour ago, it's Celia up to her old tricks again.

Mrs Riley

What is it this time? Rudeness? Laziness? Or is it being argumentative?

Val

Throwing a tin of peas at a customer.

Mrs Riley

That's different. That will be another string to her bow.

Val

The worst thing was the tin of peas was out of date.

Mrs Riley

That is shocking. *(They both laugh)* Being the only child, her parents gave her everything she wanted, especially when she started to cry and scream. Her parents did her no favours. How much do I owe you?

Val

Call it twenty quid.

Mrs Riley

It should be much more than that?

Val

I used my convenience card; it gives you twenty percent off.

Mrs Riley

You are kind. Now here I want to talk to you. Now I don't want you to be upset or to judge us.

Val

What ever is it?

Mrs Riley

Five years ago, just as Ray was diagnosed with Alzheimer's, we both decided that we wouldn't leave the other on their own, to carry on struggling through a life we don't want to be in.

Val

What are you saying?

Mrs Riley

What I am saying is after nearly seventy years of marriage, in which time we have never been apart, we don't want to carry on if the other is not around anymore. We are both in our nineties now and the world is so much more different now than when we first met and fell in love, that we can't really relate to it anymore.

Val

Yes, but,

Mrs Riley

Ray doesn't recognise me anymore and his quality of life is all but gone.

Val

But your life has plenty of quality left?

Mrs Riley

Not without the man I have loved for so long. We have never been people persons, and friends and family we did have are long gone, but we have always loved nature and it's that we will miss the most. So not to miss a summer we always planned to depart this world when the first snows arrived.

Val

How do I fit into all this?

Mrs Riley

I want you to take this key and when you see the first snow fall, let yourself in. You will find a letter on the end of our bed. I hope you will be able to make our last wishes happen.

Val

Although I wish you have second thoughts as life is so precious, I will respect your wishes.

Mrs Riley

Thank you Val. *(They embrace)*

Val walks towards the door, and with tears in her eyes, she lets herself out. Five minutes later she walks through her own door to be confronted by a letter that is on the mat. Picking it up, she sees it's from the Catholic Church. Opening the letter, she reads out loud.

Val

Dear Mrs Johnson, I am writing to inform you that after much searching, we believe we have located the person you have been looking for. If you can contact us, we will be happy to give you more information. Yours Sincerely.

Val

At last, some good news.

Will She or Won't She?

Characters

Mrs Scott

A man in his late sixties. He is owner of the Happy Convenience. Although very wealthy, even after an expensive divorce, he is a caring man who will help where he can.

Settings

Val's house

The manager's office in the Happy Convenience

Will She or Won't She?

At eight o'clock in the morning, there is a loud banging sound on Val's door.

Val

Who the bloody hell is banging on my door this time of the morning?

Celia

It's me, the coffee is getting cold.

Val

(Opening her door) Well you don't see this every day. Let me think, why is Celia bringing me breakfast? Oh, yes, it is because her tribunal is as ten o'clock this morning and she doesn't know if she will be in a job by lunch time.

Celia

I don't know what all the fuss is about.

Val

Do you think it might be because you threw a tin of peas at a customer, which cut her face?

Celia

I wasn't aiming at her, it slipped out of my hand.

Val

Of course it did, especially as you were six foot away from her.

Celia

Do you think I should plead guilty on the ground of diminishing responsibility?

Val

No, not when alcohol was the cause of the diminished responsibility.

Celia

I didn't go out last night, or the night before.

Val

I bet the landlords takings are well down. He will have to put the pub up for sale.

Celia

I must agree that shop at the corner does make lovely croissants. The butter just oozes out of it. How's your coffee?

Val

Very nice thank you.

Celia

Good friends like us should have breakfast together more often.

Val

We should now you have stopped drinking and changed your usual breakfast of six cups of coffee and twenty fags.

Celia

It's very kind of you to represent me.

Val

As though I had a choice.

Celia

Do you think you can get me off the hook?

Val

As I see it, unless divine interventions intervene, then you have a chance. But if it doesn't then you could be queuing to sign on first thing tomorrow morning.

Celia

That's all I bloody need.

Val

I suppose we could always go for insanity due to your mental health issues.

Celia

There's nothing wrong with me?

Val

Is there not?

Celia

No, there's not, I'm a person who is shy by nature and finds it difficult to make friendships.

Val

Unless someone is buying the drinks. Right, it's time we caught the bus. We don't want to be late for your own execution.

As they both walk to the bus stop, people are hanging out of windows and standing on their doorsteps wishing Celia all the best. Mrs Rogers at Number 5 gave Celia a couple of tins of peas, saying, "if they sack you aim for the balls."

Celia
That's the only trouble when you live in a close-knit community, everyone knows your business.

The bus stops and opens its doors.

Frank
Here she comes, who needs a gun when you have got a tin of peas to hand.

Val
Morning Frank.

Frank
How are you going to defend this criminal?

Val
On grounds of insanity.

Frank
I'm liking the briefcase Val, you don't see many of those around here. Would have thought a briefcase was way above your pay grade?

Val
It is, believe me. This is only for show. We might be working-class, but we are as good as everyone else.

Val and Celia both sit down.

Mrs Irons
I threw a tin of baked beans once.

Val
Did you Mrs Irons?

Mrs Irons
I did. I took it out of my carrier bag and threw it at a security guard.

Val

Why was that?

Mrs Irons

Well, everything in my carrier bag was nicked.

Val

Did you get away?

Mrs Ivans

I did. I was much younger then and the security guard was well overweight. When I got home my mother was furious.

Val

What because you had been on the rob?

Mrs Irons

No, because I had thrown the baked bean tin at the security guard. My mother wanted beans on toast for her tea. *(They both laugh)*

Val

Right come on, here's our stop. *(Getting off the bus)* See you Frank.

Frank

Good luck to you.

As they both walk into the happy convenience, many of the workers wish Celia good luck as they walked to the manager's office. They both sat outside his office. Five minutes later Sarah Viola comes out of the manager's office.

Sarah

We are ready for you now.

They all go into the manager's office. Sarah goes to sit down next to Adam Fletcher, the store manager. Val and Celia sit directly in front of the manager's desk.

Adam

Good morning ladies. As you know a few days ago Miss La-One threw a missile at a customer, hitting her in the face. Now fortunately the customer, after being given a voucher worth five hundred pounds, was happy not to proceed with any legal proceedings against us. Knowing what you did and how much it has cost The Happy Convenience to put right your wrongs, will you now resign your position at the Happy Convenience Miss La-One?

Val

Thank you Mr Fletcher for highlighting the case and your expectations for Miss La-One. However, as Miss La-Ones representative, we must turn down your invitation for Miss La-One to resign.

Adam

On what grounds?

Val

On the grounds of Miss La-Ones mental state at the time, caused by her working conditions and her state of mind at the time.

Adam

You have got to be joking?

Val

I can assure you Mr Fletcher I am not joking.

Adam

Well, if that is the case, let's discuss Miss La-Ones working conditions.

Val

On the morning of the accident,

Sarah

Accident?

Val

On consulting with Miss La-One, she has told me that the customer had asked Miss La-One if she knew where the tins of peas were. Being as the customer was in a rush Miss La-One, who had gotten to the tins of peas first, threw a tin to the customer in order to save her time. I agree Miss La-One shouldn't have thrown the tin of peas, but in doing so she showed herself as an employee who was putting the customer first.

Adam

Unbelievable.

Val

Yes she is when it comes to helping the customer's needs.

Adam

So how did her working conditions contribute to the 'accident' as you put it.

Val

Miss La-One that morning had been moved around three difference aisles within the space of half an hour. With her third move, Miss La-One found herself working alongside Mr Peters who, as you know, has hygiene issues which affected Miss La-One's judgement.

Adam

So what you are saying is that Miss La-One is innocent of the whole situation?

Val

What I'm saying is that Miss La-One did make a wrong judgement in throwing the tin of peas, but because of the situation at the time, Miss La-One's judgement was impaired.

Adam

I've heard enough of this rubbish, and therefore...

Val

Well just before you do give your verdict, I must tell you that if Miss La-One is to be found guilty, then I have the permission of the union rep to contact the union office for their permission to ballot for strike action.

Adam

Are you trying to blackmail me, Mrs Johnson?

Val

Not at all, I'm trying to see that Miss La-One gets a fair hearing.

Adam

Well, I'll give Miss La-One the justice that she deserves and that is

The door opens and Mr Scott comes in. (The owner of the Supermarket)

Mr Scott

Good morning everyone. Please don't sit down Mr Fletcher, I'm sure you don't mind vacating your chair for me.

Adam

It is my office.

Mr Scott

You are right it is, but your office is in my Supermarket, and I do pay your wages, although the way I heard you talking to my employees, you won't be getting your wages much longer if strike action is called. (Adam makes way for Mr Scott) Now Mrs Johnson, we seem to be in a dilemma.

Val

We do Mr Scott, but if I could suggest a solution to the dilemma?

Mr Scott

Please do continue.

Val

Thank you. As you know, your business is in the middle of an estate which has more than its share of hardship and poverty. Because of this, I propose that a foodbank is to be set up, which would be stocked by food that was near its sell-by-date. I'm proposing not only should the Happy Convenience supply food, but all Supermarkets in the local area.

Mr Scott

And where do you propose to set this food bank up?

Val

There is a derelict building next to the Happy Convenience car park.

Mr Scott

I hope you are not expecting me to cover the cost of work needed to restore the building?

Val

I am not. There are many who live on the estate who have had occupations such as joiners, plumbers and electricians who because of retirement or ill health have had to give up their skills, but even if it's just a few hours a day, I know these people would happily volunteer their skills to help these who suffer on a weekly basis to find enough food to feed their families.

Mr Scott

You have been doing your homework Mrs Johnson.

Val

Some things matter in life.

Mr Scott

And why do you think I would agree to your proposal Mrs Johnson?

Val

Because you are an honest and caring man.

Mr Scott

Thank you. I try to be. So where does Miss La-One fit in with all this?

Val

Miss La-One will manage the daily running of the food bank?

Mr Scott

But doesn't Miss La-One work here full time?

Val

She does and hopefully will continue to do so, part-time.

Mr Scott

And who will fund Miss La-One for the hours she works in the food bank?

Val

I'm sure someone will appreciate the dedication that she will bring with her. In fact, because Miss La-One will be playing such a major role in the community you may want to discuss on a one-to-one basis Miss La-One's plans for the foodbank.

Mr Scott

That could be a good idea.

Val

You do like Chinese food Miss La-One?

Celia

Yes.

Val

And are you free Friday night Miss La-One?

Celia

Yes.

Val

Well, that sorts that out. Is there anything else Mr Scott?

Mr Scott

I think we have covered everything.

Adam

Hold on, what about the serious case of throwing a tin at a customer?

Val

I agree Miss La-One did throw a tin of peas accidentally.

Adam

Accidentally?

Val

I think a written warning would suffice in this case.

Adam

Do you? Well, I don't think it would.

Mr Scott

I think it will be appropriate.

Adam storms out of his office.

Val

Thank you Mr Scott. I'll leave Miss La-One in your capable hands.

Val gets up and leaves the manager's office, and with her head held high, she walks out of the store.

At Long Last

Characters

The Porter
A short man in his mid-forties. He is always eager to please.

Poppy
A mix-raced woman in her mid-twenties. She was born to Elizabeth Greenwood and given to the missionaries when she was a week old.

Setting
Belvoir Hotel

Number 5 Park Road

At Long Last

At 9 o'clock on a Friday morning, Val and Celia board the 9:10 train to London. Just as they get aboard, the train starts to move.

Celia

We made that by the skin of our teeth.

Val

Who's fault is that?

Celia

Well don't look at me.

Val

So the fact that you spent half an hour arguing with the taxi driver about how much he charged, didn't have anything to do with being late?

Celia

Well, if he had gone the way I said it would have been two pounds cheaper.

Val

All that for two pounds?

Celia

I'm a single woman who lives on her own. Believe me a pound saved here and a pound saved there adds up.

Val

Right, let's sit here. I always prefer a table seat.

As they sit down the snack trolley comes into the carriage selling teas and coffees.

Celia

I could just do with a brew.

Val

Don't get too excited, it won't be tea like your grandma used to make. They never served tea in a paper cup. It had to be served in a China cup.

Celia

And you always had to wait till it had to be served.

Val
Doesn't matter how thirsty you were.

Celia
If you couldn't make a decent cup of tea. Your name was in the mud in the community.

Val
It was, and woe betide all grandmas who didn't have their husband's food on the table for when he got home from work.

Celia
And in the summer grandads would expect to see their home-grown veg on the plate.

Val
Definitely. Although my grandma drew the line when it came to cooking mussels on a Saturday night. If grandad didn't cook them himself then he didn't have them. They smelt terrible.

The trolley stops next to Celia.

Celia
I'll have two teas with sugar, and a couple packets of those sandwiches, what's in them?

Hostess
Cheese and tomato, cheese and tuna or you can have cheese and ham.

Celia
If you didn't like cheese, you would bloody starve.

Hostess
Just two teas then?

Celia
Give me a couple of packs of cheese and tuna.

Hostess
That will be seventeen pounds.

Celia
You what? For two teas and two lots of sandwiches? You are having a laugh.

Hostess
At this time on a Friday morning believe me love, laughing is

the last thing on my mind.

Val
Just pay the woman.

Celia
But.

Val
But think of your new working role, now pay her.

Celia hands over seventeen pounds.

Hostess
Thank you madame.

Celia
You will find I'm a miss.

Hostess
That doesn't surprise me. *(The hostess takes her trolley further down the carriage)*

Celia
Bloody robbing cow.

Val
She is only doing her job,

Celia
She did a bloody good job on me. Seventeen pounds.

Val
That reminds me, how did your Chinese go down with the boss?

Celia
You mean James?

Val
First name terms are we now?

Celia
We are, and by the end of the night we became much closer. He gave me a kiss on the cheek.

Val
Did he now.. is he going to support you with the foodbank?

Celia

Well, I explained what I had planned and how we would staff it and get supplies in. I also gave him a list of people's names who would help with the restoration of the building.

Val

You must have an inkling if he is going to support us or not?

Celia

The only thing he would say is he would let me know in a few days when he had thought about it and gone through the figures. Although talking about figures he was telling me that the bitch of an ex-wife of his took him for at least five million pounds.

Val

Let's hope he has still got some savings left in his bank.

Val smiles. The train pulls into Leicester train station. Five minutes later, Annie and Joan get onto the train.

Celia

Is that Annie and Joan?

Val

Bloody hell it is. *(Shouting)* Over here you couple of drunken tarts.

Annie

Would you believe it Joan, Val and Celia, I'm surprised to see you two in daylight.

Celia

What's that supposed to mean?

Annie

Well you are Dracula's daughter aren't you?

Val

You are nothing but a couple of witches you two.

Joan

(To Val) Are these two seats taken madam?

Val

Yes.

Joan

Put a spell on them both Annie.

Val

Now that we covered all the pleasantries, what are you doing on a train to London?

Annie

It's our Suzi's twenty-first tomorrow.

Val

Never. She is never twenty-one.

Annie

Yes, me youngest is twenty-one. Although how I got pregnant in my mid-forties I'll never know. Thing was though my Dan *(Annie's husband)* said "I'll put something on it" and of course I said "what at my age?"

Val

Is she still a lesbian?

Annie

She sure is. We are all going out gay clubbing tonight.

Celia

That's one thing I would have liked to do.

Annie

What?

Celia

Mix with different types of people, people with different religions, cultures, and sexualities. You don't get to experience that on our estate.

Val

You're right. It's been the same families living on the estate for as long as I can remember.

Celia

It's what they know and can relate to. That's why most girls on the estate marry guys on the estate and if they get knocked around a bit or cheated on they will always give the bloke a second chance again and again, because that's what they grew up with and that's all they know.

Val

Remember Tina at number 32?

Joan
Who could forget.

Val
She started dating Danny two doors down. Danny who was rotten to the core. Beat up women, drugs, drink and had been inside twice but like a lot of girls on the estate they believe they can change them and that they wouldn't do anything bad to them. What happened to her?

Annie
He raped and strangled her, because she said no to him when he asked to borrow some money. Those who are rotten, stay rotten.

Joan
We are going a bit deep here girls, it's the frigging weekend. What have you got in those cups?

Celia
Over-priced tea.

Joan
Right get rid of them, I've got some clean cups in my bag. *(Joan gets a bottle of Vodka out of her bag and pours it into the cups from under the table)* Here you are Val.

Val
Thanks love.

Joan
What about you Celia love?

Val
She has stopped drinking; on account she will be doing a job that needs her to be a hundred percent professional.

Celia
What you say is very true Val, but I think we should just have the one to celebrate with my dear friends on my promotion.

Annie
But.

Celia
Joan just pour me one and don't listen to these old witches. *(Filling up two more cups, they make a toast.)*

Joan

To a great unvirginal weekend.

Celia

Hoping this is the start of something amazing.

Val

To a happy twenty-first birthday.

Annie

For Val to find a daughter who needs to be told the history of where she comes from. *(They all say cheers)* Are you nervous?

Val

A bit. But there are somethings you have to do in life. A daughter should know what her mother did to save and care for so many. It's a trip I have to make to fulfil Liz's dream.

Joan

Let's toast to that.

Annie

I would do, but the small amount of Vodka you put in my cup has left me nothing to toast with.

Joan

Something's never change. Give it here. Anyone else need a top up? *(Val and Celia push their cups towards Joan)*

Annie

Cheers to Val. *(Everyone say's cheers)* Talking of memories, we have had a few.

Celia

We have, with some of the deaths of the estate being bizarre beyond belief.

Annie

Do you remember suicidal Sue?

Val

Everyday she was threatening to commit suicide.

Celia

Mind you it didn't help the fact that her husband was never very supportive.

Annie

You are right there. What with his gambling and drinking there was never much money around. She said to him "I've not even got enough money to commit suicide." He gave up drink for a week and gave her the money.

Joan

Did she use the money?

Annie

No, she put it in the purse she used to pay the rent. It was gone two days later.

Joan

Where had it gone?

Annie

In the Dog and Duck, where most of the money went that he could get his hands on.

Joan

Did she get to kill herself?

Annie

No, she never got the chance.

Joan

Why was that?

Annie

Well, because she got stuck in Betty's queue at the Happy Convenience, she had missed the first two buses already, so racing out of the Convenience the handle on the carrier bag broke, which saw all of her oranges, what had been on special offer, roll onto the road and not thinking she ran out into the road to pick them up, the bus went smack into her. She never stood a chance.

Val

In not standing a chance, was consistent throughout much of her life. Funny thing was though, when she was in her early twenties, she had the chance to be with two young men. One of them was a guy who was small and well overweight, a face for the radio. The other was a very good looking, and always knew how to have a good time, which of course is why she chose the work shy, over drinking, womanising, waste of space who had no ambition as opposed to the other guy who left the estate and set up his own business which I've heard has made the guy very rich.

Joan

Then there was Gina, who told everyone she was training to be a nurse.

Celia

She got found out when Mable at number 67 was having a heart attack and needed mouth to mouth resuscitation.

Annie

What did she say?

Celia

"I couldn't give her mouth to mouth on account of bad breath" and when poor Mable died in front of her, she had the nerve to say, "You can get toothpaste for less than a pound."

Val

No-one saw her after that. I don't know where she disappeared to.

Annie

The worst one was Mr Guy on Bonfire Night.

Joan

Was I there?

Annie

No.

Joan

Where was I then?

Annie

Some bloke's bed. I suspect, you had left school.

Joan

I'll have you know I've been with the same man for forty years, ever since I was twenty-five.

Annie

What about the ten years before that? You never went up the aisle in white.

Joan

It was off white.

Annie

Very off, more like a shade of black. *(They all laugh)*

Joan

So, what was the story of this Mr Guy?

Annie

It was bonfire night and having the name Mr Guy, it was only a matter of time before his house would catch fire.

Joan

And did it?

Annie

It sure did. Screams were heard coming from a bedroom window.

Joan

Did everyone rush out to help?

Annie

They did, but there was a slight delay as Corrie had just started and everyone wanted to know if Deirdre was going to leave Ken for Mike Baldwin.

Joan

I can see why there was a delay.

Annie

So, when Corrie finished everyone rushed out, only to find that the fire had taken hold, and Mr Guy was hanging out of a bedroom window.

Joan

Was the fire engine late?

Annie

It was, on account that nobody had phoned 999.

Joan

Why was that?

Annie

As you know the weather had turned icy cold, and with the power cuts the flames were giving everyone free heat.

Joan

Where is he now?

Annie

He went to live in Spain, they don't have Guy Fawkes night over there.

Val

Ladies, we are coming into St Pancras.

They all get off the train and start to walk down the platform.

Annie

Right, this is us. Don't forget we will be in G.A.Y tonight.

Celia

We will see you there.

Both Annie and Joan walk off in the direction of the tube, whilst Val and Celia head towards the taxi rack. Getting into the taxi, Val tells the taxi driver where he needs to go, and twenty minutes later they are outside their hotel. After paying the taxi driver, they head for the main entrance and walk into the main lobby.

Val

Bloody hell Celia, how big is this place?

Celia

The size, the décor, this is where ladies like us should be staying.

Val

How much is it a night?

Celia

The suites we are in are usually five hundred pounds a night, but if you know someone who works here, then you are below the hundred.

Val

Who do you know?

Celia

You know the guy I was talking to on the bus that time?

Val

Who? Graham?

Celia

That's right. Well, we kept in contact, and he now works here as a porter.

Val

Well, make sure you thank him.

Celia

He's been thanked more than once.

Val

I bet he has.

They both walk over to the reception.

Receptionist

Can I help you ladies?

Celia

Yes, you have a reservation for is Miss La-One and Mrs Johnson.

Receptionist

(Looking at the computer) Yes, we do. Rooms 204 and 205. Will you be requiring room service?

Celia

Yes, can you bring up the bottle of the Boulay and a bowl of strawberries and raspberries with extra thick cream. Are there any messages for me?

Receptionist

There is a letter for you.

Celia

(Being passed the letter) Thank you.

Both Val and Celia follow the porter up to their rooms. Opening the doors to their suites, the Porter takes their luggage into their rooms and, after receiving a tip, leaves.

Val

Wow, this bedroom is three times bigger than the size of mine, and the bathroom is twice as big as mine. *(There is a knock at the door)*

Celia

Come in. *(One of the porters comes inside with a tray of what Celia had asked for)* Please put it down on the table.

Porter

Will that be all?

Celia

For now. *(She gives him a tip and the porter leaves)* It might be only eleven o'clock, but I need a glass of wine.

Val

I'll pour two glasses shall i?

Celia

That would be nice.

Val

(Sitting down) Are you going to open your letter?

Celia

I forgot I had it. *(She opens the letter)* It's from James.

Val

Is it now?

Celia

He is in London and wants to meet me for afternoon tea at the Ritz. He wants to talk about my proposals for the food bank.

Val

Do you think that's the best place to talk about food banks, when you are spending hundreds of pounds just on tea?

Celia

I know what you mean, but without Mr Scott's backing, there won't be any foodbank and that's the place he wants to meet me. He's picking me up at one o'clock and its twelve o'clock already.

Val

I thought you were helping me find Liz's daughter?

Celia

I won't be that long, a couple of hours at the most.

Celia rushes off to get ready whilst Val helps herself to another glass of wine. An hour later, Celia rushes into Val's room.

Val

Are your knickers on fire?

Celia

I forgot to put any on, how do I look?

Val

I'm sure he won't say no in that outfit.

Celia

That's what I'm hoping. You don't think this tops a bit low, do you?

Val

I'm sure it will do the job it's intended for.

Celia

I'll see you later. *(Celia rushes out)*

Val

(Phoning the Porter) Could I have room service please? Five minutes? That would be lovely.

Porter

(Knocking on the door) Room service.

Val

Come in.

Porter

(Walks in) How can I help you?

Val

Are you familiar with the north of London?

Porter

Yes, I grew up in Tottenham.

Val

Oh good, I'm looking for this address, *(she shows him an address)*

Porter

Yes Mrs Johnson, I used to go to the pub just around the corner from there.

Val
> Good, how do I get there?

Porter
> You need to catch the tube to Finsbury Park, when you get outside the tube you catch the bus to Crouch End. Ask the bus driver to drop you off at Park Road.

Val
> Thank you very much.

Porter
> You are welcome.

The porter leaves the room and Val gets herself ready for her trip. Half an hour later, Val walks out of the hotel and walks towards the tube station. After paying for her tube, she gets onto the train, which twenty minutes later, arrives at Finsbury Park. Walking out of the station, she gets on the bus to Crouch End, asking the bus driver to stop at Park Road. After another twenty minutes, the bus driver shouts "Park Road". He tells Val to cross the road and it's the first on the right. Val walks across the road and comes to Park Road. Walking along the road Val stops at number five. She see's that it is a house that has been converted into three flats. Walking up to the door, she presses the top button, and a young woman comes to the door.

Poppy
> Hello, can I help you?

Val
> You can't, but I hope I can help you.

Poppy
> I'm not buying anything today, I doubt you can.

Val
> But I'm not here to sell you anything.

Poppy
> Do I know you?

Val
> You don't but I did know your mother.

Poppy
My mother died five years ago of malaria in West Africa.

Val
But your real mother died a few months ago.

Poppy
My real mother?

Val
You did know you were given away a week after you were born?

Poppy
I don't think I want to hear this.

Val
I'm sure it's a shock for you, but at your mother's funeral I was given a letter where I was given specific instructions to find you and to tell you that there wasn't a day that went by that she didn't think of you.

Poppy
I just can't take all this in.

Val
Although I'm leaving tomorrow, come and have breakfast with me, I'm staying at the Belvoir, eight o'clock alright?

Poppy
Yes, alright.

Val
I'll see you there.

Val turns and walks down the path. Arriving back at the hotel, Val goes straight to her room. Seeing that Celia has not returned, Val decides to have a quiet night in. The next morning, Val comes down for breakfast and see's Poppy waiting for her.

Poppy
Hello.

Val
Good morning, I'm glad you could make it. I'm Val by the way.

Poppy
And I'm

Val

Poppy?

Poppy

Yes, that's right.

Val

I'm glad your parents kept your name your mother gave you. Shall we go and have some breakfast?

Poppy

That would be nice.

They both walk into the restaurant where they sit on a table next to the window.

Poppy

I would love the full English.

Val

Then that's what you will have.

Waiter

Are you ready to order?

Val

We are, Miss?

Poppy

Robinson.

Val

Will have the full English and I will have the eggs Benedict, where I come from you won't find it on a menu often. Will tea be alright?

Poppy

That will be fine.

Waiter

Thank you. *(He walks away)*

Val

I hope you have recovered from your shock yesterday.

Poppy

It was a lot to take in.

Val

I bet it was. *(Taking a photograph out of her bag)* This is a works do we went on a couple of years ago. *(Pointing to Liz)* That's your mother there, her name was Elizabeth Greensmith. As you can see, there are many likenesses; eyes, nose, even your mouth is shaped the same way.

Poppy

(With a tear in her eye) How could she have given me up?

Val

Believe me, she never wanted to. Your mother was a nurse and she found herself in a situation where she had the sole responsibility of whether the weak would live or die, and if she had kept you then many more would have starved to death without your mother's help. I think that is why she called you Poppy, like the first World War, when there was death and suffering the Poppy grew to represent hope and beauty, and you were her hope and beauty amongst the death she saw each day.

Poppy

A truly remarkable woman.

Val

Very much so. She gave you to John and Alison I believe, who were missionaries?

Poppy

That's right.

Val

Did you have a happy childhood?

Poppy

Very happy. They were everything you would want as parents, kind and loving, which made my life very happy. Although they have now both gone, there's not a day I don't think about them. It would have been my mother's birthday today. She deserved many years, but life had other ideas.

Val

It usually does. So, what now for you?

Poppy

I was brought up by missionaries who went around the world teaching the word of the Lord, so I'm hoping to be able to carry on my parents work and travel to Africa once I have got enough money to do so.

Val

To be able to teach the word of God shows that you are very blessed. When are you hoping to go?

Poppy

Not for some time. Although I work two jobs, London is not a cheap place to live.

Val

Would you be ready to leave in a month?

Poppy

What do you mean?

Val

I mean, would you be ready in a month or weeks if you had the money to leave?

Poppy

But I haven't got the money, so there is no point in talking about it.

Val

But Poppy, you do have the money?

Poppy

(Tears start to stream down Poppy's face) You can't give me money, we have only just met.

Val

(Holding Poppy's hands) I'm not going to give you a penny, but your birth mother is.

Val gives Poppy a letter which contains the financial settlement.

Poppy

(Crying out loud) Thank you so much.

Val

You are very welcome. *(Standing up)* Now give me a hug. *(They embrace)* Now any more details you need to know, phone the solicitors, their number is on the top of the letter.

Poppy

I will and thank you so much.

Val

You are very welcome. Now, I must go and pack, my address is on the letter. When you get settled, send me a letter on how you are doing.

Poppy

I will.

Val walks with Poppy to the door and after another hug, Poppy leaves, waving as she goes. As Poppy disappears from sight, Celia rushes through the doors with her arms open.

Celia

I think it's love.

Val

Here we go again.

It's Monday Morning Again

Characters

Billy

A tall nineteen-year-old lad who has not had much luck in his early life. Having no father and a mother who works at night and sleeps in the day, Billy found himself on his own for long periods.

Setting

Val's back garden

The bus stop

The Happy Convenience Supermarket

The fag shelter

It's Monday Morning Again

As Monday morning is wash day on the estate for most people, Val is hanging out her washing in the back garden.

Lilian
Are you there Val?

Val
(Standing on a wooden crate, Val looks over her garden wall)
Morning Lillian.

Lillian
Congratulations on finding Liz's daughter, I heard it went well.

Val
Thank you love, I see it didn't take long for the jungle drums to start banging. I only saw her two days ago.

Lillian
You know Celia's gob. There's always someone on an estate who likes to gossip, and a bottle of wine always did loosen the tongue.

Val
She was a lovely young woman who was so deserving, hopefully she will be in Africa by the end of the month.

Lillian
That's wonderful to hear.

Molly
Ladies, have you seen the new neighbour?

Lillian
What, the ones at number 29?

Molly
That's the ones, well I was just talking to Rita.

Lillian
Who? Rita who's eldest had just been sent down for two years for robbing his neighbours.

Molly
That's the one. She said the only reason they prosecuted was because he didn't steal anything, so they didn't want the

neighbours saying their furniture was not worth nicking. Anyway, there we are having a chat when a removals van pulls up.
Well, the men opened the back and walk up to the house to see if they were in. Well ladies if you could see what was in that removal van.

Lillian
What?

Molly
Junk. In fact, the only place fit for their furniture was the tip. I said to Rita they should pile it up on the back garden and set light to it. Next minute the owner rushes out and says we are a couple of nosey cows and tells us to piss off riff raft.

Lillian
Shocking. She's no better at number 25.

Molly
Why?

Lillian
Well Nelly at number 32 said she had seen men going in her house all hours of the day and night.

Val
Really?

Lillian
Really. And on wash days her clothesline has not got a single item of clothing on it.

Molly
Disgusting. It's getting bleeding common round here.

Val
Right ladies, I've got to go.

Lillian/Molly
See you Val.

Twenty minutes later, Val locks her door and heads for the bus stop. As Val nears the bus stop, a young man in his late teens walks towards Val.

Billy
(Standing in front of Val) Give us your bag bitch.

Val

I'll give you the back of my hand if you don't move.

Billy

Give it me or I'll strangle you, you old cow. *(He puts his hand on Val's throat)*

Val

I'll show you what this old cow can do.

Val knee's him between his legs and as the teen falls back, she kicks him again between the legs. Billy falls to the floor and starts to roll around on the ground in agony. As this is happening, Bev comes running out of her garden.

Bev

You alright Val?

Val

I'm fine.

Bev

(Kicking Billy on the floor as she is talking) We don't need trash like you on our estate.

Jackie

(Running out of her gate) You alright Val?

Val

Honestly, I'm fine.

Jackie

(Like Bev, is kicking Billy as she speaks) You piece of vermin.

Billy is shouting in pain.

Bev

I'll phone the police.

Val

No, don't worry about that. The fact he has been beaten up by a bunch of mature women should be enough to change his ways. Ladies, my bus is coming down the hill, I'll see you later.

Val puts her hand out and with the bus doors opening, she gets on.

Frank

Morning Val.

Val

Morning Frank.

Frank

What's been going on here?

Val

Some young lad chancing his luck.

Frank

The way he's crying out, I think his luck has run out.

Val

Let's hope he can get it back again.

Frank

The way he is rolling around on the floor with his hands holding his meat and two veg, I don't think his luck will be changing anytime soon. *(They pass the bus stop that Celia would usually gets on)* Where is Miss La-One today?

Val

She has got a rich new boyfriend. She has swapped buses for taxis.

Frank

That must be costing her.

Val

Costing him, you mean.

Mrs Irons

Even as a child she always thought she was better than everyone else. Her mother was the same.They had to go to the best restaurants where they would tell you about every course on the menu they had. When it came to clothes, it had to have a designer label on it, making sure everyone knew the qualities when buying designer items, and when they were telling you about anything new they had brought, they used words like 'the best', 'amazing' and 'quality.' They would say 'it wasn't cheap, but if you want the best.' No wonder they were never popular, selfish cows.

Val

Right here's my stop. You have a great day Mrs Irons.

Mrs Irons

You too, my love.

Val walks into the Happy Convenience where she is met by Sarah Viola, the supervisor.

Sarah

I see you have just made it, which is more I can say for your sidekick. Where is she?

Val

You best ask your boss, give him a ring, I'm sure he'll be glad to tell you.

Sarah

You are on the information desk.

Val

That will be complaints, refunds and more complaints then.

Sarah

There's always your p45 in my office?

Val

Keep your office door open, I might just pop in one day.

Val goes to the locker room and changes into her uniform. Five minutes later she is behind the information desk.

Shelley

Val can you put a message out for till trained staff, I've just got Betty, if she goes any slower people will think she's dead. I've also got Judy whose head is about thirty thousand feet up in the clouds and I've got Celia in spirit but not in body.

Val

Alright Shelley leave it with me. *(On the tannoy)* Good morning ladies and gentlemen. We are sorry for the wait at the checkouts. Can any till trained staff please report to the checkouts and can a member of the clothing staff give assistance to a customer who needs help in getting out of a blouse which is clearly too small for her.

Harold

Excuse me.

Val

Can I help?

Harold

I brought these chicken fillets yesterday, but as you can see, they have gone a shade of green.

Val

(Looking at the chicken) They certainly have sir. I suggest you take them back to the supermarket that you brought them from.

Harold

I brought them here.

Val

Now, with a label saying Pride Foods on them, you will find that Supermarket on the next street along. I hope they keep their pride when you ask for a refund.

Not very happy, the customer walks away.

Wendy

I brought this top two days ago and when I tried it on there was a small hole on the sleeve.

Val

It looks very much to me like a ciggy burn.

Wendy

No it's not, I don't even smoke.

A woman walks up to Wendy.

Paula

Bloody hell Wendy, how long are you going to be?

Wendy

I'll be there in a minute.

Paula

Whilst I'm waiting, lend me one of your fags.

Val

You were saying?

Wendy

Piss off.

Both women walk away.

Mrs Dakin
Morning Val.

Val
Morning Mrs Dakin. What can I do for you?

Mrs Dakin
Could I exchange this birthday card for this one? They are the same price. It's a card for our Penny *(her granddaughter)* I thought she was twelve on Saturday but she's twenty-one.

Val
Well both numbers do use a two and a one.

Mrs Dakin
Just what I thought. She has invited me to her twenty first, so I should have remembered.

Val
(Opening the card) Mrs Dakin, you have written in the card.

Mrs Dakin
I know, it will save someone else time having to write a message.

Val
(Reading the card out loud) 'Happy birthday to my sweet dumpling, love form your groovy granny.' I can't see many people wanting to buy a card with that wording inside.

Mrs Dakin
You never know.

Val
(Smiling) Here you are Mrs Dakin. I have exchanged your card. You have a wonderful time at this party.

Mrs Dakin
Thank you love. *(She walks away)*

Next to come up to Val is Ricky.

Ricky
Hello Mrs Johnson.

Val

Mrs Johnson, is it? You must be after something.

Ricky

I don't know what you mean, but now you mention it I brought these white trousers to go to gay pride, but they are a bit tight around my waist.

Val

I wonder why that is.

Ricky

I've always been a thirty waist, so it must be that the manufacturer must have put the wrong sizes on the jeans?

Val

It's not the fact you have put weight on then?

Ricky

I've been this size for years.

Val

Of course you have, and what are all these stains on the back of them?

Ricky

There's no stains.

Val

It's like looking at Josephs coat of many colours. What's all these green stains down the legs?

Ricky

Well, I was walking home when some big fella jumped me and knocked me to the ground. Then when I was lying there helpless, he took my jeans off and took advantage of my virginial body.

Val

Virginial *(laughing)* why didn't you report him?

Ricky

I was going to, but when he had finished, he said could he see me again and invited me out to dinner.

Val

Another freebee then?

Ricky

Are you going to refund me?

Val

Not a chance.

Ricky

You're a witch Val Johnson.

Val

That's right, and if you don't piss off now I'll put a spell on you where every time you go out you have to buy someone a drink.

Ricky

If you are going to start talking like that I am going. *(He walks away)*

Celia comes behind the desk.

Val

Just got up?

Celia

Don't blame me. Mr Scott wanted me to do some late-night dictation for him.

Val

That's what they call it now do they? Where was the letter to, France?

Celia

I'm here to take you off.

Val

About bloody time. While I remember, now that we have had the go-ahead to convert the outer building into a food bank, have you done much advertising for workmen?

Celia

Well, I have been rather busy as you know. But I did put a card in the post office window.

Val

that will help enormously.

Celia

That's what I thought.

Val
> I think because of how busy you are, we need someone else on the team.

Celia
> That might be a good idea.

Val leaves the desk and walks towards the back of the Supermarket. On her way, she sees Annie.

Val
> You've not seen Karen on your travels?

Annie
> Last time I saw her she was heading for the fag shelter.

Val
> Thanks love.

Val goes outside and walks to the fag shelter.

Pam
> Bloody hell Val have you lost your way love?

Val
> I lost my way years ago, but with the help of this young lady I think more people are going to be found again.

Karen
> It's not everyday I'm elevated to a saint.

Pam
> There is too much goodness in this shelter, I'm off.

Val
> See you later Pam.

Karen
> So why am I the golden girl at the moment?

Val
> Karen, I want you to do me and the community a big favour.

Karen
> If I can.

Val
> I want you to take over organising and running the food bank.

Karen

I thought Celia was in charge of that?

Val

Celia couldn't take charge of her own life, never mind other peoples, lives which are seeing hunger and poverty day in day out.

Karen

Val I couldn't take on that much responsibility.

Val

Oh yes you can. Think about your own life and how you struggled to put food on the table for your younger brothers and sisters. With your dad on his next conquest and your mother confined to her bed due to her depressing state after her breakdown. Who had to take control at fifteen? You did.

Karen

I did.

Val

Who lost two stone in weight because on certain days there was not enough food to go around?

Karen

I did.

Val

And who suffered physical abuse, rape and imprisonment by men but still had the determination and strength to fight back and tell herself this is not going to be my life?

Karen

Alright, I'll do it.

Val

(*Giving Karen a hug*) Thank you.

The Great Escape

Characters

Sophie

A woman in her thirties. Like many on the estate, she grew up and still lives on the same estate. She married Jack, a hard-working man, and they have two children: James, who is four, and Lucy, who is three.

Setting

The Bus stop

Foodbank

The Happy Convenience Supermarket

The Great Escape

Having a week off work, Val is at the bus stop waiting for the bus. As she waits Billy, the young lad who had tried to rob Val a couple of weeks ago, walks up to her.

Val
Have you not learnt your lesson by now?

Billy
I have, that's why I have come to say sorry.

Val
And so you should be. Why has life got so bad for you at such a young age?

Billy
Father pissed off, my mother was a lady of the night, which left me on my own for long periods at a young age. If it was left for my mother to feed me, I would have starved years ago. So, robbing became a way of life.

Val
Did you go to school?

Billy
There was little point. Even today I can barely read or write.

Val
Not much in the way of work then?

Billy
There is not much hope with my qualifications. I suspect my name will be on a prison door soon.

Val
But if you were given a chance?

Billy
Who's going to give someone like me a chance?

Val
I am. You know we are setting up a foodbank.

Billy
I had heard.

Val

Well, the woman who is in charge will need fit young guys like you to help her.

Billy

She won't want me.

Val

How are you going to know if you don't go and see her?

As she finishes her sentence the bus comes down the hill. Stopping, the doors open.

Frank

Everything alright Val?

Val

Everything is fine. Can I have two for the Happy Convenience please. *(Getting the tickets, Val turns around)* We haven't got all day.

Frank

I'd do as you are told lad. Remember last time.

Billy gets onto the bus and goes to sit with Val.

Mrs Irons

I don't know how you have the strength for someone that age.

Val

Strength in mind Mrs Irons, if not in body.

Mrs Irons

I had a young man once.

Val

Did you?

Mrs Irons

I did. Five minutes on the bed, I got cramp in both legs.

Val

I bet that was painful?

Mrs Irons

It was, but not as painful as having to watch my toyboy nicking all my stuff and me unable to move. I stuck with older men after that.

Val

Right, this is our stop.

They both get off the bus and head for the old buildings next to the Happy Convenience. Karen is standing at the door.

Karen

Hello.

Val

What is happening here? Where have all these people come from?

Karen

I put that we needed help on social media and all week people are asking if they can come and help.

Val

I knew you were the right woman for the job.

Karen

Go and have a look inside?

Val

Wow.

Karen

As you can see, the sinks are in, the gas and electric are connected. The kitchen will need a couple more days to be up and running though.

Val

So, when will you be ready to open do you think?

Karen

If we carry on like this then we should be opening in two weeks. Who's your friend?

Val

This is Billy, who is nineteen and in need of some purpose in life.

Karen

Where do I fit in?

Val

I want him to be your right-hand man.

Karen

 Are you sure?

Val

 Very sure.

Karen

 Okay. Right, is it Billy?

Billy

 It is.

Karen

 Right, I want you to finish off the painting above where the cooker is going to be. When you have done that, you can make a start washing all the plates and dishes that people have donated to us.

Billy

 Leave it with me.

Val

 It's a good idea having a kitchen. You all will be able to add to the food that will be donated. Right, I must go or Viola the wicked witch of the west will have my guts for garters.

Val hurries towards the Happy Convenience entrance, where she is met by Sarah Viola.

Sarah

 I see you are five minutes late. Have you gone down to part time and not told anyone?

Val

 I've not, but if I do, you'll be the first to know.

Sarah

 Remember who you are talking to.

Val

 I always do, that's why you never hear my thoughts.

Sarah

 I'm quite happy for you to hear my thoughts. You are on clothing this morning.

Val

 That means I'll be watching over-weight customers trying to

squeeze into sizes that they have not been for years then.

Sarah

I want you back in five minutes.

Val rushes to the locker room and after changing into her work uniform, she appears at the clothing section, where she is confronted by an elderly man trying a pair of trousers on.

Val

Excuse me Sir, this is not the place to be trying trousers on.

Customer

Well, if you had kept your changing rooms open, I wouldn't be doing this now.

Val

I know what you are saying, but the other customers don't want to see a man's underpants. Especially when they have red love hearts all over them.

Customer

They attract women to me.

Val

I'm sure they do Sir, among other things.

Customer

(With the new trousers on) What do you think?

Val

They do look a bit short on the legs.

Customer

Yes, but they show my white socks off more.

Val

I'm still not sure, are they for a special occasion?

Customer

I haven't brought any trousers for years and as it's my ninth birthday next week I thought I would treat myself.

Val

Good for you. Why shouldn't you wear love heart underwear with white socks at ninety.

Customer
They do attract a lot of female attention, are you free next Wednesday?

Val
You will have to excuse me. I can see a lady having problems trying on a blouse. *(She rushes off)*

Customer 2
Help.

Val
I'm here Miss, you seem to have got a bit tangled up, let me help you.

Customer 2
I don't know why it won't go over my head, I've always been a medium size, I think they have labelled it wrong.

Val
Do you think so?

Customer 2
I do. I'm always very careful what I eat. If I have a packet of crisps, I always have the low-fat ones.

Val
How many packets do you eat a day?

Customer 2
Because they are low fat, about five or six? And if I have a packet of biscuits then I only have half the packet at a time.

Val
(Sarcastically) It must be the labelling.

Customer 2
I knew I was right. Even if I have a plate of chips, I have a salad with it. And even when I make myself a cup of tea, I only have three spoonfulls of sugar instead of the usual six.

Val
How many cups do you have a day?

Customer 2
Anything between seven or eight.

Val
There is another customer waiting. Good luck in getting the right size. *(Under her breath)* You will need it.

Two small children walk towards Val.

Lucy/James
Hello Aunty Val.

Val
Hello you two, come and give me a hug *(they both hug Val)* where is your mother?

Lucy
She is looking for shoes for James. Mum says his feet are growing too fast.

Val
James you will have to stop growing.

James
I keep telling my feet not to grow Aunty Val, but they don't listen to me.

Val
We will have to get them some hearing aids. *(They all laugh)*

James and Lucy's mother walks up to Val.

Sophie
Hello Val. *(They both hug each other)*

Val
You spending your money again?

Sophie
With these two my purse is never shut and as for Jack, he never stops working. He must be doing twenty hours a week overtime. I never see him.

Val
It will all be worth it in the end. One day the kids will be adults and you two will be with each other 24/7

Sophie
Lets hope it's not too soon. *(They both laugh)*

Val

Have you got James' shoes?

Sophie

I have but they are a little bit expensive.

Val

Don't worry about that. Go and get some for Lucy as well.

Sophie

Val I have to save up first.

Val

Lucky for you, I have, now go, and get some.

Sophie

Val, but.

Val

No buts, now move yourself. I will be back in ten minutes, I'm just off to the loo and don't worry about the price.

Sophie and the kids head towards the shoe rack. Val walks to the toilet and on the way, she bumps into Rose.

Rose

Can you smell smoke?

Val

They have probably burnt the bread again. If i don't get to the toilet it will be floods we have to worry about not fires.

Val reaches the toilet and as she sits down, she can hear screams coming from outside.

Val

(To herself) What the bloody hells going on?

Two seconds later, there is a big explosion. As Val finishes having a wee, she rushes out to see that there are plumes of black smoke everywhere, with the flames hitting the ceiling.

Celia

(Shouting) Val!

Val

(Rushing over to Celia) I'm here! What's happened?

Celia

Flames were coming out of the ovens when all of a sudden, the drinks aisle exploded.

Val

I don't expect it's looking too good up that end?

Celia

Let's hope there was not that many people buying booze.

Val

We have got to go and have a look.

Celia

Are you mad!

Val

Maybe, but if there is a chance of saving someone?

Celia

The firemen must be on their way.

Val

Every minute counts. Come on!

Both Val and Celia walk slowly through the thick smoke. On their way, they see a couple of people lying on the floor. Val goes to see if they are alive.

Celia

Any sign of life?

Val

Not as I can see. Come on, lets move on.

They both reach the end aisle, where they can see Annie and Joan lying on the floor.

Celia

(Screaming) Are they dead?

Val

No, but they are not looking too good. We have got to get them out of here. *(Val looks around, afraid)* Get these two trolleys over there and stay down.

Celia

(Bringing over the trolleys) Val we have got to get out, the

flames are getting higher.

Val

Help me lift them into the trolleys.

Two minutes later, both Annie and Joan are in the trolleys.

Celia

Come on!

As they both head towards the door, one of the trolleys goes over a bump.

Val

What was that?

Celia

Who cares? We have to get out!

Val

Hold on, it's a woman.

Celia

Who is it?

Val

(Kneeling down) It's Sarah!

Celia

Is she dead?

Val

No, but she looks in a bad way.

Celia

We have got to go.

Val

We can't leave her here!

Celia

We can!

Val

Help me put her on the bottom of my trolley.

After both struggling to put Sarah on the trolley, they head off towards the exit. Five minutes later, through the thick smoke they can see some people standing at the exit.

Karen

It's Val and Celia! *(Everyone cheers)*

As Val and Celia reach the outside the entrance, the ambulance crew rushes to take care of the injured.

Sophie

(Coming up to Val with tears streaming down her face) Val, I don't know where Lucy is!

Val

What do you mean?

Sophie

I was holding them both when Lucy broke free saying she wasn't leaving without her new pair of shoes.

Val

I'll get her.

Val heads towards the exit, Karen and Shelley try to stop her.

Shelley

Val, you can't go back in there! You are going to die!

Val

If I don't try, I'll die inside if anything happens to her.

Val rushes back into the store. By now, the whole store is a blaze with thick black smoke making visibility very difficult. It takes Val twenty minutes to reach the clothing section which is fully alight. Val keeps shouting Lucy's name, but there is no answer. As Val gets to the shoe aisle, she can just see the outline of a child on the floor. Rushing over, she kneels. As she does so, Lucy lifts her head.

Lucy

Aunty Val, can I have these shoes?

Val

You can have any shoes you want, now let's go and see mummy.

Celia

(At the exit) It's been over half an hour and there is still no sign of her.

Shelley
Give her another five minutes then we will have to go in.

Sophie
(Walking up) Any sign of them?

Shelley
Not yet.

Sophie
Please let them both be safe. What am I going to do without my little girl. *(She begins to cry uncontrollably)*

Shelley
Hold on, I can see something!

Sophie
Is it them?

Shelley
It is! *(Everyone cheers)*

Lucy
Mummy, do you like my new shoes?

Sophie
(Holding Lucy in her arms) They are beautiful, just like you.

New Beginnings

Characters

Sharon
A medium sized woman in her late thirties. She is the mother of Billy. Having started having sex at an early age, she made it into a career, picking up many clients over the years, because of this everyone on the estate has backlisted her.

Setting
Outside Sharons house

Foodbank

The Happy Convenience

New Beginnings

It is Friday morning, and Val is pegging out some washing.

Lillian

(In her back garden) Molly, are you there, love?

Molly

(Coming out of her back door) I'm here Lil, what's up?

Lillian

I've just looked out of my bedroom window, and I can see Val hanging out some washing.

Molly

On a Friday?

Lillian

I know. I always thought Friday was dusting, hoovering, and doing the food shopping.

Molly

So did I. Do you think the fire the other week has made her forgetful?

Lillian

Well, there's got to be something not right. Before we know it she will be doing her washing on a Sunday.

Molly

If that happens then we know she's gone mad.

Lillian

I'm going to go have a word with her. Val, are you there love?

Val

(Looking over her wall) Hello Lillian.

Lillian

Is everything alright love? Are you feeling alright?

Val

Yes, I'm fine. Don't I look well?

Lillian

We were just wondering why you were hanging washing out on a Friday.

Val

I'm trying to get the smell of smoke out of my work uniform. This is the third time I've put it in the washer.

Lillian

Now we understand. We thought the fire had left you a bit unbalanced.

Val

I'm fine.

Lillian

How many died?

Val

Only the two. It was lucky there was only two. It could have been a lot worse.

Molly

Well, it could have been six if you hadn't been so brave.

Val

I'm sure I did what anyone else would have done.

Lillian

(Looking at Molly) I'm not so sure.

Molly

Did you hear old Bill has died?

Val

Has he?

Molly

Every time I saw him, he would say 'I've not got long to live.'

Lillian

He hadn't, he's dead now.

Molly

I was just hoping he could have had a bit longer.

Val

Why?

Molly

He was going to put some shelves up for me. I'm going to have to pay someone to do it now. It has put me out a bit.

Val
When's the funeral?

Molly
It's next week, but I'm not going.

Val
Why?

Molly
His family has got in the same caterers who did George's wake at number 59. The food wasn't that good. I had to go to the chippy after, I was still hungry.

Lillian
How are those three women that you saved getting on?

Val
They are all out of hospital now. Annie and Joan were treated for smoke inhalation and Sarah Viola did receive ten percent burns and a concussion caused by a flying brandy bottle.

Molly
Well, it was the right bottle.

Val
Why's that?

Molly
You always have brandy when you aren't well.

Lillian
You must be unwell twenty-four-seven.

Molly
How dare you. *(They all laugh)*

Lillian
Have you heard anything from Mrs Edwards?

Val
I'm going to visit her tomorrow. I've heard she isn't very well.

Lillian
For her to just collapse like that in the middle of putting her washing out was frightening to see.

Molly

It was a good job she was hanging her washing out Monday morning or she would have been lying there for days.

Lillian

Do you think she well ever come out of the nursing home?

Val

I doubt it, especially as that low-life husband of hers has pissed off again taking all the money.

Lillian

That one's rotten. Give her my love when you see her.

Val

I will.

Lillian

So, what are you up to today?

Val

I'm off to the opening of the foodbank. After that we are being given a sneaky look at the new Happy Convenience before it opens.

Molly

Is Celia still seeing the boss?

Val

Last time I saw her, she was saying their relationship was going from strength to strength.

Molly

I bet her need for his money is going from strength to strength too?

Val

Well, I did hear she's put on an Oscar winning performance when it comes to telling everyone how brave she's been.

Molly

I wondered why the gold was mounting up on her fingers.

Val

Right, I better go and get ready.

Lillian

You enjoy your day.

Half an hour later Val comes out of her front door and walks down the street towards the bus stop. On her way, she bumps into Billy's mother.

Val

Hello Sharon.

Sharon

Hello Mrs Johnson.

Val

I hear your Billy has turned into a shining star.

Sharon

It's about bleeding time.

Val

Do you ever regret not having more time to help Billy when he was growing up?

Sharon

It would have been nice, but you know how it is. Bills have to be paid.

Val

Could you not have found another job?

Sharon

I could, but it would not have paid as well. There are many people around here who do not approve of me giving my body to men for money, but when you are trying to keep a roof over your head, I had no choice. Although, with my lack of education, sex is one of those things I'm good at. Yes, to leave your child alone for long periods is wrong, but I had nobody to turn to. Family and friends shut the door on you when you do the job that I do.

Val

I can understand the dilemma you had, but at the end of the day there is a nineteen year old lad out there that wants his mother's love.

Sharon

I can't turn back the clock.

Val

True, but you can try and make up for it now by showing him you care.

Sharon

How do you expect me to do that?

Val

Take an interest in what he is achieving. Tell him how proud you are as his mother?

Sharon

I'm sure he knows that.

Val

Does he? It's the opening of the foodbank today, why don't you come with me and see the hard work he is doing?

Sharon

I don't think that will be a good idea.

Val

Why not?

Sharon

I sleep in the day and besides, people don't want to associate with the likes of me.

Val

I think you can forgo a couple of hour's sleep and I'm very happy to be seen with you. The bus will be here in five minutes.

Sharon

But...

Val

No buts, come on or we will miss the bus.

Both Val and Sharon head towards the bus stop. On their way, people who usually talk to Val either just wave or avoid eye contact. As the bus stops, the doors open, Val gets on first and pays for Sharon's fare.

Sharon

You didn't have to do that?

Val

You're right, I didn't, but I wanted to.

As they go to sit down, passengers on the bus look at Val with disgust on their faces.

Sharon

You don't have to go through this for me.

Val

I'll put myself through anything if it helps a son to reconcile with the past and give him a happier future.

Mrs Irons

I was offered money to give an older man oral sex once, of course, I was much younger then.

Val

(Loud voice) Did you Mrs Irons?

Mrs Irons

I did. It was the easiest twenty quid I ever made.

Val

Right, this is our stop.

As they both get off the bus, they are confronted by a large crowd that has gathered in front of the foodbank.

Sharon

They are all looking at me.

Val

Let them look. Remember why you are here.

As they join the crowd Mrs Scott stands at the front to make a speech.

Mr Scott

Ladies and gentlemen, it is so nice that you have come out today in order to support the residents who are struggling. I would like to thank all the people who have volunteered their services to transform a derelict building into a building that will help many people who are fighting day to day to feed their families. I must give a special thank you to Karen Miller, who with her determination and hard work, has made this building ready for the community to use. I would also like to give a big thank you to Billy, who has done everything that has been asked of him, even staying through the night to get things finished. It is rare to see such a hard-working lad at such a young age. Please accept these gifts as a big thank you for all your hard work. *(Everyone applauses)* Finally, there is one person who I and everyone in this community would like to say a huge thank you to. Not only was the foodbank her idea, but through her bravery and determination, three ladies and a child wouldn't be here today. Mrs Johnson, please step forward. *(Val walks to the front of the crowd to a loud applause)* Mrs Johnson, everyone on the estate thanks you for all the help you have given to the estate over the years, and on a personal note, I want to thank you for the hard work and dedication you have given to the Happy Convenience. Thank you!

Mr Scott hands over a present to Val (a golden bracelet) and gives her a hug.

Val

Thank you so much. *(Waving to the crowd)*

Mrs Scott

Now, I would like Mrs Johnson to cut the ribbon.

Val

(With scissors in hand) I am very happy and proud to declare the foodbank open. *(Cutting the ribbon, everyone claps)*

Mr Scott

Thank you Mrs Johnson. Now everyone, as you know a few weeks ago the Happy Convenience saw a terrible and devastating fire which brought with it a huge amount of damage. However, I was determined to rebuild it and make the Happy Convenience the centre of this amazing community. So, although we don't open until Monday, I want you all to come in and get used to the changes that have been made. Please follow me everyone.

Leading the way, Mr Scott takes everyone into the Happy Convenience. As they all walk off, Val and Sharon stay behind.

Val

I think there is someone who wants to see you.

Sharon

(Turning around she walks straight up to Billy and gives him a massive hug) I'm so proud of you. Who would have thought my son has now become a respectable and well-liked part of the community. You have really changed your life around.

Billy

Stop it mum. It's because of Mrs Johnson's help that I am enjoying life again.

Val

(Walking over) That's what happens when you give people a chance in life. Karen, have you got a minute?

Karen

(Walking over) Hello.

Val

Have you met Billy's mother?

Karen

No, I've not. It's nice to meet you. *(They shake hands)* You must be so proud to have a son who works so hard and is appreciated by so many.

Sharon

Believe me, I am very proud. It's not everyone who can change their life around.

Val

Talking of changing their life, did you need someone to do a couple of shifts at the foodbank?

Karen

(Looking at Val's face for guidance) I did, but it would have to be someone who could not only evenly distribute food out, but someone who is a good listener and can advise people on a lot of problems they might be having. I need someone who knows what it's like to be poor and have empty cupboards. A person who understands what physical and mental abuse is all about and succumbing to a man's is needs in the bedroom, no matter how depraved his demands are.

Sharon

(With a tear in her eye) I have all those qualifications.

Karen

Then we need you.

Val

Didn't I hear that people with a counselling qualification are in short supply?

Karen

You did, but there are even less people who are qualified from the estate. People who have first-hand knowledge of the problems people are facing on a daily basis.

Val

There is no substitute for experience.

Sharon

Why are you telling me this?

Val

Because all estates need someone like you to fight the corners of poverty and abuse.

Sharon

I left school without any qualifications. I was making too much money to care about getting an education.

Val

Don't they do a two-year access course which leads onto university?

Karen

They do, the course starts in October.

Sharon

You are not listening to me. I have no qualifications.

Val

You have the qualification of life experiences. Now that's a qualification every college course needs. Leave it with me, I'll find out about enrolling.

Sharon

But you aren't listening.

Val

You mean, you're not listening to all those women who are crying out for help. Billy, take your mum and show her all your hard work.

Billy

Come on mum, I'll give you the guided tour.

Sharon

But...

Billy

Come on mum. *(Taking his mum by the hand, he leads her off to look inside the foodbank)*

Karen

She is just the person that is needed around here.

Val

She sure is. Right, come on, let's look inside the new Happy Convenience.

Karen

Do we have to?

Val

The bills are saying we should.

Both Val and Karen walk into the Happy Convenience. They see Annie and Joan standing together.

Annie

Here comes Saint Val.

Val

Hello ladies, how are we girls?

Joan

Thanks to you, we are fine.

Annie

I see La-One has arrived.

Joan

I hear she uses a map these days to find the place.

Val

That's what happens when you have a rich boyfriend.

Annie

I hear he is peeling her grapes for her these days.

Joan

I'm sure he is not drinking the wine for her though.

Karen

Not a chance of that. *(They all laugh)*

Mr Scott

Ladies and gentlemen.

Annie

Not another speech?

Mr Scott

Thank you for all coming. I do hope you like what we have done with the place. The changes to the lay out I'm sure will help both the staff and our customers.

Annie

It don't matter what the layout is, we still have to fill up the shelves.

Mr Scott

Now as you know this supermarket has always been the first love of my life, until I started dating a beautiful woman who has knocked the Happy Convenience off the top spot.

Joan

Was Specsavers shut. *(They all laugh)*

Mr Scott

So, with a new store, a new love, and surrounded by so many friends, this is the best place to ask.

Val

He's not.

Annie

He can't.

Mr Scott

Celia, have you got a minute?

Celia

(Walking forwards) What is it?

Mr Scott

(Going down on one knee, and lifting a diamond ring up) Will you marry me?

Celia

(With a big smile) Yes!

Goodbye to Old Friends, Hello to New Love

Characters

Tony
A medium sized man in his mid-sixties. He has been a teacher for the last thirty years and although he has retired, he still does a bit of supply work.

Milly
A small woman in her mid-fifties. She is a senior carer at the Guest Residential home.

Brian
A tall man in his sixties. He is Judy's husband of thirty years. He has his own business.

Setting
The Guest Residential Home

Sharon's house

Judy's house

Goodbye to Old Friends, Hello to New Love

At around nine o'clock in the morning, Val can be seen walking into the Guests Nursing home, where she is met by a member of staff.

Milly
Can I help you?

Val
Yes, I'm here to see Mrs Edwards.

Milly
Are you a relative?

Val
I'm her next-door neighbour.

Milly
Val, is it?

Val
Yes.

Milly
She said you would be coming to see her.

Val
How is she?

Milly
Not very well I'm afraid. Have you got a minute?

Val
Yes. *(They walk into Milly's office)*

Milly
The other day Mrs Edwards was complaining of her arm hurting, so we took her to the hospital for an x-ray. What the x-ray revealed was a fractured arm and a lot of old breakages that seem to stem back from many years ago. Do you know how these could have happened?

Val
By marrying the wrong man.

Milly
Don't tell me her husband is responsible?

Val

I'm sure she did have some accidents over the years. But I would say that most of them were by her drunken waste of space husband.

Milly

Why did she not leave him?

Val

To go where? She married at a time when a man was always believed to be right. You could argue as much as you wanted, but the man's word was final. Even her family, although sympathetic, would not interfere and divorce was looked upon as shameful throughout the extended family.

Milly

Was he always like this?

Val

No. At first, he showed himself a loving, hard-working husband. But when he lost his job, alcohol found its way in, which led to the house keeping money disappearing on many occasions.

Milly

A pretty miserable existence then?

Val

Yes.

Milly

But it is her mental state that is the most concerning. It's as though she is getting ready to die. She just stares into space for much of the day.

Val

Let me have a chat with her. You never know, I might pull her out of her depression.

Milly

Let's hope so.

Milly leads Val into the residence room, where Mrs Edwards is staring out of the window.

Val

Hello Mrs Edwards. *(She carries on staring)*

Milly

I'll leave her with you. *(Milly walks away)*

Mrs Edwards

(Turning to face Val, and in a soft voice) Hello Val, I knew you would come.

Val

Of course, we have been neighbours for many years. How are you my love?

Mrs Edwards

I'm ready Val, I knew when they took me out of my home last week it would be the last time I ever see it again.

Val

Surely not?

Mrs Edwards

My last battle is nearly fought, and it is one I won't win. I'm afraid the mental and physical pain I have had to go through over the years have caught up with me. I'm in my eighties now, and it's time I wasn't here.

Val

But Mrs Edwards,

Mrs Edwards

Not buts my dear friend. Now I want you to do me a couple of favours.

Val

Yes, of course.

Mrs Edwards

Firstly, I want you to take my plants and look after them. I have had some of them for years, they have become a bit like family. Secondly, over the last couple of years a stray cat comes to see me each night and of course, I can't let him starve. I've called him George. He never comes into the house, but he does sleep in my shed in the winter. Finally,

Val

I thought you said I couple of favours?

Mrs Edwards

I did, but I'm a woman in my eighties who is ready to start her next adventure. So, I'm sure you will allow me to have one more.

Val

Of course I will.

Mrs Edwards

Under my bed there is a loose floorboard. Now, if you lift it up, you will find a black box. The money you find in there, I want you to donate it to the foodbank. There were many times we had to go hungry over the years and as you know it was no fun. Next to the money you will find a small blue bag which has five gold souvenirs in it. I want you to sell them and buy a plane ticket for yourself.

Val

I can't accept that. Who will look after the plants and the cat?

Mrs Edwards

I'm sure you will get a lodger or rent out your place, so the cat and the plants will be well looked after. I've told you before, leave the ghosts of the past behind you, you have a lot of living to do yet my girl.

Val

(With a tear in her eye, she gives Mrs Edwards a big hug)
Thank you.

Mrs Edwards

I don't want any tears, I have had some happy times in my life which I am very grateful for. I would have liked to have seen more places abroad, but you are going to do that for me. Now off you go and don't look back, just keep looking forward. Goodbye, my love.

Val

Goodbye, Mrs Edwards.

Knowing that she will not see her neighbour for many years again, Val walks out of the 'rest home' with tears streaming down her cheeks. Later in the day, Val and Karen are knocking on Sharon's door.

Karen

(Shouting through the letterbox) Your next two clients have arrived!

Both laughing, Sharon opens the door.

Sharon
Very funny. Can I help you ladies?

Val
Yes, by getting out of that dressing gown and putting something smart on.

Sharon
Why would I do that when I've been up all night?

Val
Because it is time you turned your life around.

Sharon
How am I going to do that?

Val
By coming with us. Your interview is at four.

Sharon
I know we chatted the other day, but I didn't take it seriously.

Val
When desperate women need your help to survive, you better take it seriously.

Sharon
I don't think it's a good idea.

Karen
We do. So, get up them stairs and get changed.

Sharon
Or what?

Val
We will tell the council and the DHSS that you are living off immoral earnings.

Sharon
You bitch.

Val
You better believe it. Now get up those stairs.

Sharon reluctantly goes back up stairs whilst Val and Karen go into Sharon's living room.

Karen

Bloody hell, even Dracula wouldn't want to live here.

Val

Open them curtains.

Karen

(Opening the curtains) How much dust is in here?

Val

She must have the whole estates dust.

Karen

(Writing in the dust) Clean me!

Val

I bet her last name is Havisham, her in Great Expectations. Although I don't think her place was this bad.

Karen

What about the kitchen?

Val

Unless you brought a gas mask with you, I wouldn't bother.

Sharon

(Walking into her living room) What do you think?

Val

Sharon love, you are not auditioning for a porn movie, you're being interviewed to be accepted onto a counselling course. So get back upstairs and put a longer skirt on.

Karen

And put a bra on at the same time.

Sharon goes back upstairs.

Val

Let's go, I'm having breathing difficulties.

As Val and Karen reach Karens car, Sharon comes out of her house and walks towards the car.

Karen

You look rather virginial in that outfit.

Sharon

Some of my clients like this look.

Val

Surely they don't think you are Snow White? *(They all laugh)*

Karen

Right, come on, let's get in.

Karen gets in the driver's seat with Val besides her. Sharon gets in the back of the car.

Sharon

I don't think I should be doing this.

Val

A few hours ago, I went to see my next door neighbour in a rest home, and because she didn't have someone like you to help her with the mental and physical abuse she went through over the years, she ended up in a rest home wanting to die. How many more women are crying out for help, but nobody hears them?

Sharon

Alright, that's told me.

Val

And if you get onto this course your lifestyle has got to change. It's no good becoming a councillor if nobody wants your help because of what you do. I know Karen wants you at the foodbank, so she will fit your shifts around your course, and Billy is working there now so there should be enough money coming in to pay the bills.

Sharon

They probably won't want me anyway.

Val

Tell them the truth, and who knows.

Karen

Right, we are here.

Val

Good luck!

Sharon gets out of the car and walks to the reception.

Karen

Do you think she will be accepted?

Val

She has only got herself to blame if she doesn't.

Karen

Before I forget, I got a message from Judy.

Val

What does she want?

Karen

The party begins at seven, and don't bring any booze with you.

Val

I forgot all about that. Judy always has a party at this time of the year, so she can get rid of some of the duty-free booze she stores up. It gives her an excuse to go on holiday and get some more to replace what everyone drinks.

Karen

That sounds like a good night.

Val

It would be if the morning didn't follow. Why don't you go as my plus one?

Karen

Is Celia not going?

Val

Now she is marrying a millionaire, she will probably be spending the night at the Savoy or jetting off to the south of France.

Karen

Did you hear she is finishing work next week?

Val

It doesn't surprise me. Why work when you don't have to? Not as though she ever did work.

Karen

Here she comes, lady of the night.

Val

She looks as though she is in shock.

Sharon

(Walking to the car) Val, they have accepted me!

Val

Congratulations! A new start and a new you.

Sharon

Val, they accepted me? Why?

Val

Because you are going to succeed and now you need to believe that too. Right Karen let's get this student home, she is going to need the rest of the day to cancel all her clients and clean her house from top to bottom.

Half an hour later, they reach Sharon's house.

Sharon

Thank you both so much.

Karen

(Sharon getting out of the car) Sharon?

Sharon

Yes?

Karen

Can you do Monday and Tuesday at the foodbank?

Sharon

I can.

Val

That's good. It's just that Karen will be recovering.

Sharon

Leave it with me.

Sharon shuts the car door and walks into her house. Ten minutes later, Karen stops outside of Val's house.

Val

Right, this is me.

Karen

What time shall I pick you up?

Val
Get the taxi here for eight.

Karen
I've got the car.

Val
If you don't want to wrap the car around a lamp post or better still, lose your licence, then I'll see you in the taxi at eight.

Karen
Okay.

At eight o'clock in the evening, a taxi pulls up outside Val's house. Seeing the taxi from the window, Val comes out of her house and climbs into the taxi where Karen is sitting on the back seat.

Val
Evening love.

Karen
Hello Val. What am I letting myself in for?

Val
The mother of all hangovers. Driver, can you take us to Alexander Close?

Karen
Is that the posh side?

Val
It is. Judy's husband owns a successful security company.

Karen
Is that why they can afford to go on holiday a lot?

Val
Yes. Her wages pay for all the holidays.

Karen
It's alright for some.

Val
That's what you get if you pick the right husband.

Karen
Talking of relationships. I did something very stupid the

other day.

Val

Like what?

Karen

No, I can't say.

Val

Come on girl, spit it out.

Karen

Keep it to yourself, but me and Billy kissed. I know it was stupid, but it just happened.

Val

And who's to say it shouldn't have happened?

Karen

He is fifteen years my junior and on this estate. I could be his mother.

Val

But you're not. Stop the self-doubt and just run with it and before you say, 'what will other people say', who gives a toss.

Karen

But we are at different stages of our lives.

Val

Believe me love, what that lad has done and seen, I don't think he would ever want to see those early stages again.

Karen

But I want children, and my clock is starting to tick.

Val

I think he would make a very good dad, but don't rush into that side of things, keep taking the pill because if you rely on a bloke to just put a condom on or pull out just before he reaches his climax, then you will be stuck with kids,

Taxi Driver

It was the opposite for me. I picked this girl up at a club and took her back to mine. As I was worse for wear, I trusted her to put a condom on mine and she didn't.

Val
Did she not?

Taxi Driver
No. It turned out that she wanted a house, and becoming pregnant the council got her one.

Val
All I'll say Karen love is take your time and listen to your feelings. You do like him then?

Karen
Yes, a lot.

Val
(To the taxi driver) Are we there yet? I can hear the music; she must have got DJ Dan back again. He always holds the mic to his mouth so you can't understand a word he is saying.

The taxi driver pulls up on the drive. Val pays him and with Karen, she gets out of the taxi.

Karen
Is that someone lying on the lawn over there?

Val
Probably. Looks like Judy has started everyone on the shots already.

Karen
(Walking into the house) Bloody hell, how big is this place?

Val
That's money for you. But if you were brought up on an estate it's hard to leave it, even if you can afford to.

Karen
Why's that?

Val
Familiarity, understanding, speaking the same language. That's what makes people feel safe.

Judy
Here she is! *(Judy gives Val a hug)*

Val
Hello love. You have got loads of people here already.

Judy

I would like to think it was because of my hosting skills but the greedy gits are only here for the booze. Talking of booze, what are you having?

Val

Just a small one.

Judy

Wash your mouth out with soap. Anything smaller than a double and there's the door. Come with me love, that's you as well Karen.

They both follow Judy into a large room which contains a bar.

Karen

How much drink have you got? There must be hundreds of bottles.

Judy

(Going behind her bar) Val, you still on the gin?

Val

Yeah, what flavours have you got?

Judy

Every flavour.

Val

I'll have Rhubarb.

Judy

Do you want some tonic?

Val

Yes, lots.

Judy

(Pouring the gin out of sight of Val) Here we are love.

Val

Bloody hell Jude, how much did you put in it?

Judy

Don't worry, it's mostly tonic.

Val
> *(Tasting it)* Wow, did you put any tonic in?

Judy
> Karen what you having?

Karen
> Have you got any Disaronno?

Judy
> The last count, we had ten bottles of it. What do you want with it?

Karen
> Coke and ice please.

Judy
> There you are love. *(Passing Karen her drink)*

Karen
> How big is the glass?

Judy
> Right, I must play my hostess with the mostess part. The girls are out in the garden, but watch out for Pam. She was last seen doing the conga, solo, around the garden and Karen, a young man has been asking for you.

Karen
> I don't know who that could be?

> *Both Val and Karen head towards the garden. On the way, various people say hello and hug Val. They reach the garden.*

Annie
> Here she comes.

Val
> Hello ladies. *(They all go over and hug Val)* What you drinking?

Annie
> I'm on the Malibu. But it is my third glass so I'm not expecting to be on my feet for much longer. (They all laugh)

Val
> Rose, what you drinking?

Rose

(Slurring her words) I haven't got a bloody clue. *(She falls to the ground)*

Shelley

There goes another one.

Val

Did I hear Pam is doing the Conga?

Annie

She was but collapsed in the vegetable patch about half an hour ago. I don't think Judy's tomatoes will win any prizes this year. It's a good job she booked next week off as she is going to be in a vegetative state for the next few days. *(Everyone laughs)*

Karen

You have to be here to believe it.

Shelley

It's a good job it's a six-bedroom house.

Val

There's usually at least three to every bed by twelve.

Karen

Are they?

Val

No love. They couldn't manage it if they tried. That's where Judy and her husband put those who have collapsed.

Judy

(Holding a tray) Here we are ladies, you have not had your shots yet.

Annie

Do we have to?

Judy

We need to toast our Val. Everyone to Val! *(Everyone raises their glass)* Everyone get another one? *(They all do)* To Karen for doing an amazing job at the foodbank! To Karen!

Everyone

To Karen!

Judy

I see Rose has collapsed. Brian! *(Judy's husband)*

Brian

What?

Judy

Can you sort Rose out for me?

Brian

(Shouting) Tony, can you give us a hand?

Brian gets Rose's arms and Tony gets her legs.

Judy

Put her in the back bedroom, the others are getting a bit full. *(They both carry Rose off)* Thanks love. Right, I must keep circulating. By the way Karen love, that person who was asking about you is in the orchid at the bottom of the garden.

Val

The plot thickens. Don't just stand there, go and have a look.

Karen walks towards the orchid. As she approaches, she can see a man standing there with his back towards her.

Karen

Excuse me, I hear you have been looking for me? *(He turns around)*

Billy

I've been looking for someone like you all my life.

Karen

Billy? What are you doing here?

Billy

Now that I'm a respectable member of the estate, I got an invite. *(Handing Karen a glass of champagne)* A toast to us.

Karen

I told you that kiss was a mistake.

Billy

Was it? (He kisses her) Was that kiss a mistake too?

Karen

No.

Watching both Karen and Billy from behind a tree, Val smiles and walks back towards the house.

Judy

Is everything alright?

Val

Everything is fine. Who was that Tony fella? I've not seen him here before.

Judy

He moved onto the estate about a year ago. Messy divorce, she got the house.

Val

Any children?

Judy

Three, but they are all grown up now. You find that a lot in couples.

Val

What?

Judy

When the kids grow up and leave, couples find it was the children that were the glue to them staying together. I'll tell him you were asking about him. *(She walks away)*

Val

Don't you dare.

Shelley

I'm starting to see two of everything. I can't wake up in one of Judy's beds again, I'm going whilst I can still walk. See you later.

Val

See you later Shelley.

Annie

I'm going to the toilet. I could be gone a while.

Val is standing on her own. Tony comes up behind Val.

Tony

We can't have you standing on your own.

Val

(Turning round) Hello.

Tony

I've brought you a drink. Rhubarb gin alright?

Val

Thank you, how did you know I was drinking rhubarb gin?

Tony

I would like to say I'm a good judge when it comes to what a woman likes to drink, but Judy gave it to me saying your glass was empty.

Val

Your glass is never empty for long at Judy's parties.

Tony

I'm Tony by the way.

Val

I'm Val.

Tony

I hear you are a bit of a hero around these parts.

Val

Not really. I was just in the right place at the right time. I heard you are divorced.

Tony

Not much stays secret around here I see.

Val

If you live on an estate, nothing is secret for very long.

Tony

I've been divorced for about two years now. When the kids grew up and left, we discovered there was nothing that we had in common anymore. Are you married?

Val

I was, but he died about eight months ago. Heart attack.

Tony

I am sorry, do you have any children?

Val

I had a daughter, but she died just after her twenty-first birthday.

Tony

That must have been terrible.

Val

It was, but she had various complex issues. She did amazing to live as long as she did. Are you still working?

Tony

Just about, but I do, a little supply teaching now and again. Do you work with Judy?

Val

I do at the Happy Convenience. Although I am thinking about leaving.

Tony

To do what?

Val

To live abroad and travel to places I have always wanted to see.

Tony

Sounds amazing. Are you free next Friday night?

Val

I don't think I have got anything planned.

Tony

I'll pick you up at seven.

Val

I'll look forward to it.

Judy

Val, your taxi is here.

Tony

I'll walk you to your taxi.

Val

Thank you.

Val and Tony walk through the kitchen to the front garden, they go through the double gates. Tony opens the taxi door.

Tony
Good night.

As Tony closes the door, he stands watching the taxi drive away.

A New Lodger for Val

Setting

Val's back garden

Foodbank

The Happy Convenience

Italian restaurant

A New Lodger for Val

Val is in her back garden and is shouting over the wall to Lillain.

Val

Lillian, are you there?

Lillian

(Rushing out of her back door) Is it spitting? I must get my washing in.

Val

No, it's not raining. The home that Mrs Edwards was in phoned me yesterday telling me she has passed away in the night.

Lillian

Bless her. It was expected but it always comes as a bit of a shock. *(Shouting)* Molly, are you there?

Molly

(Running out of her door) Is it spitting?

Lillian

No love, Mrs Edwards has passed away.

Molly

That's sad, she was such a nice woman.

Lillian

What's going to happen to the house?

Val

Well, by rights that nightmare of a husband still owns it, but whether he comes back again or not, who knows.

Lillian

Let's hope he never comes back.

Molly

Talking of death, Mrs Henry at number 19 was telling me that she knew a woman who just before she died said to her husband; 'Don't leave me up in heaven on my own for long' and had left various things on the bed for him to commit suicide with.

Lillian

That's shocking. Did he use any of them?

Molly

No. The last she heard he's become a bit of a playboy; enjoying wine, woman, and song.

Lillian

You get worse. Have you been in the house?

Val

She wanted me to have all the plants, so I popped round last night to get them. She also wanted me to feed the stray cat that comes to see her.

Molly

Is it that moth eaten one?

Val

I've not seen it yet.

Molly

Well, if it is, it looks like it's not had the best life.

Val

That's probably why Mrs Edwards started to feed it; she could relate to the suffering.

Lillian

And that poor woman did suffer.

Val

Right, I'd better go. I'll let you know when the funeral is.

Lillian

Make sure you do.

An hour later Val steps off the bus and heads for the foodbank. As she approaches, she see's a young woman standing at the back of the wall.

Val

Excuse me, are you alright? *(There is no answer)* Excuse me? *(Val walks around the back of the wall where she sees a woman in tears)* Now then, what's all this about?

Lady

I never thought I would have to go in a place like this.

Val

Well, that's the same thought many other women have had.

But life never works out the way you plan.

Lady
I've always managed to put food on the table and clothes on the back of my children, but I can't do it anymore without help.

Val
That's why this place was set up, to give people like yourself the help that you need to get through these tough times. We have got food to feed your family and workers who have the knowledge to get you the money that you need to survive. Come with me, I know just the person to help you.

Lady
But I feel ashamed.

Val
Never forget you are as good as anyone else. Now come with me.

They both walk through the doors, where they are met by Karen.

Karen
Hello.

Val
I've got a young lady here who needs some help.

Karen
Well, you have come to the right place. Sharon, you got a minute.

Sharon
(Walking over) What's the problem?

Val
I've got a young lady who is in need of some help.

Sharon
We all need that from time to time. Believe me love, I've been there. Come on love, there's a little office space over there. We will get you sorted. *(They both walk off)*

Val
She is a totally different woman.

Karen

She is going to be an amazing councillor.

Val

Now the reason I'm here is I am bearing gifts.

Karen

That sounds amazing.

Val

Not as you knew her, but my next door neighbour of many years died yesterday.

Karen

I am sorry.

Val

She wanted me to donate the money she had saved over the years to the foodbank.

Karen

That is so kind of her.

Val

Her worthless husband was always stealing her housekeeping money but she managed to save five hundred pounds, which I don't know how she did it, but she did.

Karen

That's wonderful. This money will come in very handy. Do you know what?

Val

What?

Karen

I'm going to get one of the retired workers on the estate to make a plaque with her name on. That way, everyone will remember her.

Val

What a lovely idea. Right, I'm going to have to go, the Viola is back. Everything alright with you and Billy?

Karen

Everything is fine.

Val

And party night?

Karen

Let's just say it is a good job I remembered to take my pill.

Val

That's good to hear. I have got to go. *(Val rushes to the door)*

Karen

Val!

Val

What?

Karen

Did you say gifts?

Val

Bloody hell, I did. *(Rushing back)* I brought you a cupcake to show you that we are all thinking of you.

Karen

(Smiling) Thank you.

Giving Karen a hug, Val rushes out of the door and up the path to the Happy Convenience. As she goes through the main entrance Sarah Viola is standing with her arms crossed.

Sarah

Well, I see some things never change. Ten minutes late. It seems to me while I've been away that employees think they can waltz in at any time and expect to get their full wage at the end of the month. Well, I'm back.

Val

It's good to see you back Miss Viola and looking very well.

Sarah

Don't try and soft soap me. What is your excuse this time?

Val

I was helping to get a young woman's life back on track.

Sarah

Anymore of that and I will be helping you get your P45 back on track. You're on tins and frozen.

Val
>   Why both?

Sarah
>   The La-One was supposed to be on frozen, but can you see her
> anywhere?

Val
>   No.

Sarah
>   Exactly. I want to see you working in five minutes.

*Val rushes off to the locker room and gets her overalls on. She
is back within five minutes.*

Customer
>   Excuse me Madam, can you tell me why these tins of beans
> have only got two days left to their sell-by-date?

Val
>   Because of this they are marked up at half price.

Customer
>   But I want to use them at the weekend, which means they will
> be out of date.

Val
>   If that is the case sir then I suggest you buy a tin that is well in
> date.

Customer
>   But they are twice as much.

Val
>   Because you have twice as much time to eat them. If you'd like,
> I can get a supervisor to help you?

Customer
>   No don't bother, I'll have a tin of tomatoes instead.

The customer walks away and Annie walks towards Val.

Annie
>   Some customers are hard work.

Val
>   That one definitely was. Especially when tins of tomatoes are

double the price of beans. But the customer is always right.

Annie
We know different. Don't look now, but there is a man coming towards us holding a newspaper which is covering his face.

Val
Who do you think he is?

Annie
He could be some mass robber or someone who kidnaps vulnerable women and makes them their slave.

Val
What books have you been reading?

Annie
I'm going to fetch security.

The man comes up to Val.

Val
Can I help you sir?

Tony
(Dropping his newspaper) Yes you can, by not forgetting I'm picking you up at seven.

Val
(Smiling) Seven it is.

Tony
These are for you. *(He gives her a bunch of flowers)*

Val
Thank you.

Tony
I'll see you later. *(He walks off)*

Annie
Am I missing something? Who was that?

Val
He's a friend I met at Judy's party.

Annie
I don't remember him?

Val

I'm not surprised, you spent half the night in the toilet.

Annie

I was sick as a dog. The worst thing was though seeing all that free booze in the toilet.

Val

That does piss you off. I saw Pam half an hour ago, she seems to have gone a shade of red on her face?

Annie

Well, you know when she was doing the conga.

Val

Yes.

Annie

And she fell into Judy's tomatoes?

Val

Yes?

Annie

Well, it's the dye off the tomatoes. She has scrubbed her face that many times.

Pam

(Pam comes round the corner) Can someone help me with this labelling machine?

Val

(Val puts up her hand) How. *(They all fall apart laughing)*

Sarah

What is going on here? We are supposed to be working, not fooling around. Now get back to work.

Val

I would love to, but I finish at one. I'm meeting the boss's girlfriend at two for a late lunch.

Val walks off to the locker room and hanging up her overall, she rushed out of the store. Catching the sixty-four bus, she arrives in town twenty minutes later. Getting off the bus, she walks through the Victoria Centre where Celia is waiting for her at the clock.

Celia
Hello love. *(They both hug)*

Val
Could you not manage coming into work today?

Celia
Just didn't have the time. I thought we would go Italian. I fancy a bit of pasta, come on I'm starving.

Val
You are holding onto a few designer carrier bags there?

Celia
Now we are engaged, I am having to buy a whole new wardrobe of clothes. The places he takes me demands that I look my best. Here we are, is it getting colder or is it me?

Val
We are into September now.

Pedro
Good afternoon, Miss La-One.

Celia
Hello Pedro. I think we will have a table by the window.

Pedro shows them to their seats and gives them some menu's.

Pedro
What would you like?

Celia
I'll have the carbonara. What about you Val love?

Val
I think I'll have the same.

Pedro
Anything to drink?

Celia
We will take a bottle of the Piedmont.

Pedro
Thank you.

Celia

Now, I've not told anybody but we are going to have an engagement party at the beginning of December, not sure where yet, but I'll keep you informed.

Val

Do you think this might be the one then?

Celia

Do you know Val, after all these years I can honestly say it is. I'm too old now to be on the singles market.

Val

So, his money is not a factor?

Celia

You know where we have been in life Val, growing up with very little money, having our mothers saying no to us if we wanted something like a new toy or some clothes, because you didn't want the other kids to look down on you.

Val

I remember in the winter there was more ice on the inside of my bedroom window than on the outside. I must have had at least six blankets on my bed. The hot water bottle didn't stay hot for long.

Celia

But in those days Val the winters were so cold, and the summers were hot, but we never seemed to get as many illnesses as people do nowadays. If you did then there was always someone on the street who knew what to do or advise you what medicine to take. You weren't ill for long and as for our mothers they just soldiered on regardless. It didn't matter how ill they were. So, to answer your question, money is a factor. Nobody wants a life where you just exist.

Val

Are you going to sell your place?

Celia

Now that, I'm not sure. I won't be doing anything until I've got a ring on my finer. If anything goes wrong from now until next spring, I'll still have a roof over my head. You know as well as I do Val, trusting and relying on a man is fraught with dangers, even if he is nearly seventy. Although, I must admit, using someone else's credit card does make you feel good. Especially when I'm buying things I could never afford before.

Val

This pasta is good.

Celia

It is, and the wine is not bad either. *(Looking out of the window)* is it me, or are there people begging on the streets over there?

Val

I'm afraid there is. With the cost of living going up and services that could help people in desperate need of money, more people are finding that the streets are becoming home.

Celia

It must be a terrible situation to be in. That woman who is sitting on the pavement asking for money, don't we know her?

Val

(Looking closely out of the window) I don't think so.

Celia

Isn't it that woman who threw her husband out for cheating on her, but she found out he hadn't paid any of the bills for months, so the bank evicted her?

Val

It can't be?

Celia

It is, it's Carol.

Val

You're right, it is. I've got to go and help her.

Val rushes out of the restaurant and crossing the road, she kneels in front of Carol, who has her head down and doesn't see Val.

Carol

Can you spare a little change please?

Val

I can spare you more than just change.

Carol

(Looking up and seeing Val, Carol bursts into tears) I've got nothing Val, nobody wants to know me.

Val

Lucky for you, I do.

Carol

I'm so embarrassed.

Val

We are all two pay cheques away from the streets, so don't be. I've got a three-bedroom house, with two empty beds. So, get yourself up and I'll flag a taxi down.

Carol

You don't want a loser like me around?

Val

You're right, I don't. But I do want a winner around me. So move it.

Val flags down a taxi and half an hour later, they are both walking through Val's front door.

Carol

This is nice.

Val

I'm glad you like it. Now, I've put the immersion heater on, so go and run yourself a hot bath and I'll leave a dressing gown on your bed and by the looks of you, you need a hot meal inside you. Off you go.

Carol

Thank you Val.

Val

Go, I'm putting the oven on now.

While Val goes into the kitchen, Carol goes upstairs and runs herself a hot bath. After half an hour, Carol walks down the stairs wearing the dressing gown Val put on the bed.

Carol

That was lovely Val.

Val

Right sit yourself down, I've done you a steak and kidney pie with lots of veg. You have got to get your strength up.

Carol

Thank you so much.

Val puts the food on the table and sits down next to Carol.

Val

How did you get in this mess?

Carol

By trusting a man not to cheat and to pay the bills. When the bank took my house, I went to stay at my mothers, but as you know our relationship has never been very good. Two months later she died and as she was only renting the council took the house back.

Val

There must have been others who could have helped you?

Carol

After the first couple of people said no, I was too ashamed to ask anyone else. When the money ran out the streets was the only place left to go. I'll pay you back Val.

Val

You're right you will. As you might have heard, Celia has hit the jackpot with her boss so there will be a job going. I'll get you an interview.

Carol

No-one will want me.

Val

Let's hope that they do because these bills don't stop coming. On this estate you work, or you fall.

There is a knock at the door.

Carol

Is that someone knocking at your front door.

Val gets up and opens the door.

Tony

(With flowers and chocolates) Good evening, are you ready?

Val

Tony, you are going to hate me for this, but I can't come out tonight.

Tony

Are you dumping me before we even got started?

Val

No, it's just that something has happened and I need to stay in tonight.

Tony

Well, if that's how you feel it's best that we don't go out.

Tony turns and storms off down the path. Val comes back into her house.

Carol

Please tell me that I have not stopped you from going on a date?

Val

No, you are fine. Somethings are more important at the moment. Besides, if he wants me, he'll try again.

Carol

He would be a fool not to.

The Power of Love

Setting

The Happy Convenience Supermarket

Mr & Mrs Riley's house

The Power of Love

Val walks through the main doors of the Happy Convenience.

Sarah
Ten minutes early, couldn't you sleep?

Val
I'm sleeping well thank you.

Sarah
You must be after something?

Val
Well, now you mention it, there is something I need to ask you.

Sarah
I thought so. If you are looking for time off, forget it. Christmas is in sight.

Val
It wasn't that.

Sarah
Well, what is it then? I haven't got all day.

Val
Now that Celia is leaving, will there be a vacancy for a job?

Sarah
There could be, depends on who it is?

Val
I've just taken in a lodger who needs a job, and seeing as we are good friends, I thought I would ask.

Sarah
Good friends, don't push it.

Val
It was thinking friends when I was saving you from the fire. A fire that could of killed many more than it did.

Sarah
I know I'm going to regret this. Tell her to come to my office tomorrow morning at ten.

Val
She will be there.

Sarah
Right before you ask me anything else you are on till one. You have got five minutes to get there.

Val rushes off and five minutes later she is at till number one.

Shelley
Morning Val.

Val
Morning Shelley love.

Shelley
I've heard you have taken in a lodger?

Val
It was either do that or leave her on the streets, the winters are very unforgiving.

Shelley
I can see why so many rough sleepers take to the bottle. It keeps the body warm.

Val
But messes up the mind.

Shelley
It's a shame there are not more saints like you.

Val
I don't know about saints. We might live on an estate but there are some good and honest people who live on them.

Shelley
What time is your tea break?

Val
At nine.

Shelley
I'll get someone to take you off then.

Val
You are a star.

Shelley walks away and Val has her first customer.

Customer
Good morning.

Val
Good morning. Looking at all this drink, are you having a party?

Customer
Not really, I thought I would stock up for Christmas.

Val
It's nice to see a man planning ahead.

Customer
I have to. The wife only lets me touch her when she's had a few drinks and with three days off, I'm planning on getting a lot.

Val
(Giving the customer his change) Thank you.

The customer walks off.

Shelley
Did I hear that conversation right?

Val
You did. Even if I was paralytic, I couldn't manage that one.

Shelley
Neither could I.

On the loudspeaker, code two is heard. (Meaning that something urgent is happening) As everyone turns around to see what is happening, a man is seen running towards one of the exits behind one of the tills.

Val
Shelley, trolley.

Shelley gets hold of the trolley and pushed it towards the fleeing man. All of a sudden, the trolley hits the man's legs, and he goes flying into the air, falling into a heap on the floor. Everyone claps and cheers. Shelley takes a bow.

Annie
Here comes security, late as always.

Val
> I don't know why we have them.

Annie
> Look at that one, what chance has he got in catching anyone with that amount of weight on him.

Val
> With his massive belly swinging from side to side, there's not much chance of him catching anyone.

Annie
> And looking at the bloke on the floor, he must be in his seventies.

Security Guard
> Thank you ladies, but we didn't need your help.

Annie
> Looking at your stomach you need all the help you can get.

Security Guard
> What's that supposed to mean?

Val
> Shelley, I'm off for my break.

Shelley
> Alright, see you in a bit.

Although Val doesn't smoke, she heads towards the fag shelter where Rose is sitting.

Rose
> I thought you had given up?

Val
> I did years ago. I thought I would have a breath of fresh air, but it's like fog in here. I don't know how people can afford them.

Rose
> They can't but would love to. Living on an estate it's hard to find the will power to stop, especially the stresses and strains living on one brings.

Val
> I agree.

Judy

(Coming into the fag shelter) Val, can I have a word?

Val

Yes, fire away.

Rose

I'll leave you with it.

Val

See you later Rose.

Judy

What's this I heard that you didn't want to go out on your date with Tony?

Val

It's not that I didn't want to, I did, but circumstances arose where I couldn't.

Judy

What circumstances were those?

Val

You remember Carol who got her house repossessed?

Judy

The woman with a disaster of a husband?

Val

That's the one. Well, I found her in town yesterday begging on the streets.

Judy

She must have been in a bad way?

Val

She was. So, I brought her home with me. With two empty bedrooms I couldn't let a woman I've known for years sleep on the streets.

Judy

Didn't you tell Tony this?

Val

I was going to, but he stormed off.

Judy
He did, did he? You leave him to me.

Both women walk out of the fag shelter. Judy walks off to the lockers whilst Val goes back to till number one.

Shelley
Welcome back. What time you on till?

Val
I'm finishing at twelve, I don't want to leave my new lodger on her own for too long.

Shelley
I hope she appreciates you.

Val
I'm sure she does. *(Shelley walks away)*

Ricky comes to the till.

Ricky
Morning.

Val
Morning Ricky. You don't look very happy?

Ricky
I don't know what to do. *(Ricky starts to get tearful)*

Val
Ricky, whatever is it?

Ricky
You know when I told you I had been to gay pride and was walking through the park and this man took advantage of me, pulling me down on the grass?

Val
Hence the grass stains on your trousers, the trousers you tried to bring back and get your money back from.

Ricky
That's the one. Well, I've been seeing quite a lot of him recently and he asked me if I want to be his boyfriend.

Val
What did you say?

Ricky

Yes.

Val

So, what's with the tears?

Ricky

I found out yesterday he is HIV positive. Why is it I had to find out by someone else and not him?

Val

There may be a very good reason.

Ricky

Like what?

Val

If he had told you, you might have reacted like you are doing now, or he wants you so much he can't risk you saying no when he asked you to be his boyfriend. Have you been tested?

Ricky

No, I'm too scared too.

Val

Leave it with me, I'll make an appointment for you.

Ricky

Thank you.

Val

I'll let you know when it is.

Ricky

You are coming with me?

Val

I'll be there to hold your hand. See you later.

Shelley

Have you done?

Val

I have for today. I'm going to go home, put on the fire and make myself a nice cup of tea. I might even watch an afternoon film.

Shelley
That sounds bliss. They have forecast snow, so don't hang around.

Sheila comes to take Val off.

Val
Hello Sheila, you don't look to happy?

Sheila
I went out the other night to a fancy-dress party. I was dressed as a policewoman.

Val
Was you?

Sheila
I was. As I was walking down the street, a cop car came racing down the street and stopped. Two police guys jumped out of the car and arrested me.

Val
Why was that?

Sheila
They thought I was the woman who was impersonating a policewoman in order to steal money. It took me half an hour to convince them I was just going to a fancy dress party.

Val
Next time, you should go as a nun. With your luck, you could do with some divine intervention. *(They all laugh)*

As Val gets off the bus to near where she lives, flakes of snow start to fall from the November sky. All of a sudden, Val stops dead, an expression of fear moving across her face, she starts to run to Mr and Mrs Riley's house. Ten minutes later, Val arrives at the Riley's door. Val finds the key and lets herself in.

Val
Mrs Riley?

With the house still silence, Val looks around each of the rooms downstairs and finding nobody, she ascends the stairs.

Val
Mrs Riley?

With still the sound of silence, Val opens the main bedroom door and sees Mr and Mrs Riley lying on the bed in each other's arms, with their faces touching as they looked into each others eyes. Their long and loving lives had come to an end. Although tearful, Val was comforted by the looks of serenity she saw on their faces. At the bottom of the bed was a letter, just as Mrs Riley had said there would be. Opening the letter, Val reads it aloud:

My darling Val, although our time has come to an end, don't be sad for us. We both lived the life we wanted and was blessed that we could do it for over seventy years. True love is an amazing thing, and to have it for so long I thank God for his kindness for keeping us together for so long. Now Val, our solicitor has all the information he needs to fulfil our wishes, and I'm sure he will be contacting you soon. There is one wish however, that I hope you can fulfil for us. In the country park there is an oak tree that stands high up next to the old quarry. It has a beautiful view and it's where we had our first kiss. We would like you to bury our ashes there. I hope you can do this for us. Goodbye my love, and Val, the world is waiting for you.

Alice & Ray

With tears in her eyes, Val walks out of the bedroom and makes her way to the front door. A few days later, Val is walking down her stairs and sees a letter on her carpet. Picking it up, she can see its from Ray and Alice's solicitor. Opening the letter, Val reads that she has been left the house. Sitting down on the stairs, she speaks out loud.

Val
Thank you so much, you wonderful people.

There's Always Hope

Characters

Duncan

A small man in his late seventies. He is the nasty, abusive husband of Mrs Edwards

Gary

A very handsome gay man in his mid-thirties. His boyfriend is Ricky. Gary is HIV positive.

Settings

Val's House

City Hopsital

Foodbank

The Happy Convenience

There's Always Hope

It is early in the morning and Val is having her breakfast at the table. Carol is still in bed. There is a loud knock on the door.

Carol

(From her bed, shouting) Is it the bailiffs? Don't take my things. No go away, Leave me alone! *(She starts to scream)*

Val

(Rushing upstairs to Carol's bedroom) Carol it's alright love, it's not the bailiffs, you were just having a nasty dream.

Carol

Val, will this nightmare ever go away?

Val

Give it time love. I'd better go and see who's at the door.

Val goes downstairs and opens the door.

Duncan

Hello Val.

Val

Well well well, what brings trash like you to my door?

Duncan

You don't have to be so nasty.

Val

Don't I? it was your wife's funeral two weeks ago, where were you?

Duncan

I couldn't face it.

Val

Was that because you felt guilty of the way you treated her for so many years?

Duncan

We had some good times.

Val

What? In between the beatings , beatings that you left her body broken and bruised? You are a cheating, lying, thieving tosser.

Duncan
You will be glad to hear then that I have got terminal cancer.

Val
Normally, with a low life like you I would say yes. But it means that that poor woman who you constantly abused for so many years can't escape you, even in death. Go and crawl back under your stone and never come to my door again. *(Val slams the door)*

Carol
(Eating her breakfast) Bloody hell, you didn't hold back.

Val
He has had that coming for years. Right, what's the time?

Carol
Just gone nine.

Val
What are you up to today?

Carol
I thought I would do a little washing then go to the job centre; they must have a job for me somewhere.

Val
Bloody hell, with what has been going on I clean forgot.

Carol
Forgot what?

Val
You have an interview at ten with Sarah Viola at the Happy Convenience.

Carol
Now she tells me! I'm not going to make it in time.

Val
Yes you are. Right, get up them stairs and get dressed, I'll phone a taxi.

Carol
But,

Val
No buts, move yourself.

Carol runs upstairs and puts an outfit on from Val's wardrobe. Ten minutes later, the taxi pulls up.

Carol
Is that the taxi?

Val
Yes, you better be ready?

Carol
(Rushing down the stairs) What do you think?

Val
You look better in that outfit than I ever did. Right, here's a tenner, eight quid for the taxi and two quid for the bus home. Now off you go and good luck!

Carol rushes out of the door and into the taxi. An hour later Val is standing outside of the City Hospital. Ricky walks towards her.

Ricky
I don't know if I can do this.

Val
You can, you can't go through every day thinking have I or haven't I.

They both walk into the reception and Ricky gives his name and date of birth to the receptionist.

Receptionist
Please take a seat.

Both Val and Ricky sit down in the waiting room.

Val
You said your date of birth in a low voice.

Ricky
I'm gay, and if there is one thing that gays will keep to themselves or lie about is their age. Weight is another big issue in the gay world. That's why the gyms are full of gay men, trying to get a body that someone younger will find attractive. Vanity is big in the gay world.

Val

So, are you still seeing this bloke?

Ricky

I saw him yesterday and we ended up having a massive row. He tried to tell me that he didn't tell me because he didn't want to lose me and that he was on meds all the time he was with me. But I was so enraged that I was passed listening.

Val

So, you have finished with him then?

Ricky

Not exactly.

Val

What does that mean?

Ricky

It means that I love him and can't see my life without him.

Val

Right.

Ricky

But he mustn't know that as he will think he has the upper hand.

Nurse

Ricky Richards.

Val

Right, off you go.

Ricky

Do I have to?

Val

Yes, you do. What will be will be. Now shift yourself.

Ricky and the nurse walk off together as Val sits on her own watching people coming in and out the waiting room. All of a sudden, out of the corner of her eye, she sees a young lad sitting on his own at the back of the waiting room. Val walks over to him.

Jamie

What you looking at?

Val

I'm looking at a lad who doesn't look very well. Haven't I seen you before at the foodbank?

Jamie

You might have. What's it got to do with you?

Val

I have friends who work there. Do you know Billy Clark?

Jamie

Yeah, we used to hang around together but then he got lucky and found people who could help him get out of the mess he was in.

Val

Why don't you let someone help you?

Jamie

Look lady, I'm HIV positive, I drink to keep me warm on the streets and my family has disowned me. On cold nights I become a rent boy so I can go back to theirs and keep warm. I make sure the sex lasts for at least two hours.

Val

I can see you are a bit angry at the moment. But next time you are at the foodbank ask for Karen, she will sort you out.

Val walks back to her chair just as Ricky walks towards her.

Ricky

I'm negative.

Val

That's great to hear, now give me a hug. *(They both hug)* Now I don't know what the love of your life looks like, but as I was looking through the window, I saw a very handsome man looking worried.

Ricky

If it's him I'm not going near him.

Val

Come on, I've got to get to work.

As they walk out of the entrance, a handsome looking man comes towards them.

Gary

Ricky, I'm sorry. I should have told you.

Ricky

Yes, you should. If you had I wouldn't have had to go through an agonising wait for my results.

Gary

But I thought I was going to lose you.

Ricky

Why should I ever trust you again?

Gary

Because I love you.

Gary opens his arms and Ricky walks into them.

Val

Well, so much for keeping your distance. I'll see you later.

Ricky

Thank you.

Val walks off and arrives at the foodbank ten minutes later. Walking through the door, Karen walks towards her.

Karen

Hello. I've not seen you for a bit?

Val

What, with deaths and new lodgers I've been rather busy.

Karen

Full on then.

Val

Just a bit. The reason I've popped in is I've just been talking to a young lad who I think needs a bit of help.

Karen

What's his name?

Val

Jamie. He used to hang around with Billy.

Karen

(*Shouting*) Billy.

Billy walks over.

Billy

What's up?

Karen

Val says she has been talking to a lad called Jamie. Do you know him?

Billy

I do, we used to hang out a bit. He does have quite a few issues though.

Val

Like what?

Billy

He was being abused physically by his father and sexually by his uncle. When he was at school, he would sleep on the streets regularly to escape his tormentors. He often would sell his body in order to eat. He became dependant on alcohol and started to dabble in drugs. He found himself in hospital on a few occasions when he was caught by the people he was trying to rob.

Val

How old is he?

Billy

I think he is around eighteen.

Karen

Leave that with me. I'll keep an eye out for him.

Val

Inform Sharon, she is his best bet.

Karen

I will do.

Val

Right, I'd better go. I can't be late again.

Val leaves the foodbank and walks through the main entrance of The Happy Convenience. Sarah Viola is standing at the entrance.

Sarah

Only five minutes late today. I supposed I should be grateful that you want to turn up at all, what's your excuse this time? Don't tell me, saving the world.

Val

If I was saving the world, I might be half an hour late.

Sarah

And you would still expect me to turn a blind eye.

Val

How did Carol get on this morning?

Sarah

Well, she was five minutes early which was a good start. She answered all my questions and seemed very eager to find out how things are done. Although the outfit she wore seemed to be a bit tired and outdated. But apart from that she had a good interview.

Val

So apart from her tired, outdated outfit, did you give her the job?

Sarah

Not as it is any of your business, but you can tell her she is starting on Monday.

Val

I'm sure she will be most grateful.

Sarah

So she should be.

Val

Where do you want me?

Sarah

I could think of a few places, but as Miss Day has been tied up in her personal life, you'd better go on the deli.

Val

Right, I'm on my way.

Two minutes later, Val is behind the deli counter with Pam serving customers.

Pam

I've not told anybody this, but I'm going to finish work at Easter.

Val

Are you?

Pam

Yes, I'm ready. These last few months I've been starting to feel tired. It's starting to become a huge effort for me to come into work. Do you know Val, I started work at sixteen and I'm seventy in a couple of months? I think I deserve to retire and put my feet up.

Val

You do deserve it. In fact, everyone who gets to that age deserves to take it easy and enjoy what time they have left.

Pam

In our day nobody put money into a private pension.

Val

That's true. Every penny was accounted for. There was no money left to put into a pension.

Pam

When you're young, words like retirement and savings were words that were associated with older people.

Val

The thing is though; times goes so quick and before you know it you are at our age.

Pam

I've got no mortgage and I've always paid my contributions, so I should get a full pension.

Val

You cut your cloth accordingly. Every year you defer your pension the government are rubbing their hands together. The more pensioners who die the less money they have to pay out.

Customer

Excuse me, is there anyone working behind this counter?

Val

We are here to serve you Madam.

Customer

I'm a Miss.

Val

Of course you are. How can I help you?

Customer

I would like ten slices of turkey please.

Val

(Cutting the turkey) Is it for a special occasion?

Customer

A very special occasion. It's Tabitha the cat's birthday and I thought I would give her and her friends a birthday tea.

Val

That's so thoughtful of you.

Customer

It is isn't it. I always like to give them a treat for their birthdays and at Christmas of course. They are so worth it.

Val

Here we are Miss. *(Giving the customer her turkey)*

Customer

Thank you. *(The customer walks away)*

Val

Some of the families on this estate are lucky to have turkey at Christmas.

Pam

The children need to come back as cats.

Val

And the money she spent on that turkey would feed a family for at least two days.

As Val stops talking, loud screams can be heard in the supermarket.

Pam

What the bloody hell is going on?

Val

Pam will you be alright for a few minutes?

Pam

Yes, I'll be fine.

Val rushes to aisle two where she see's Jenny laying on the floor with her four children around her. A security guard is standing over her.

Jenny

(Screaming) Don't touch me!

Val

(To the security guard) Leave her alone, get your hands off her. Jenny, what's happened?

Jenny

(In floods of tears) I'm going to get evicted. They are going to take my children away from me.

Val

No one is taking your children away.

Jenny

Where am I going to live? I've got nothing.

Sarah

Come on we can't have you lying on the floor, you are putting the customers off.

Jenny

I've got nowhere to go.

Val

Yes, you have. Come on kids, you are all coming with me. Annie, can you get my coat.

Annie

I'll go and get it.

Sarah

(To Val) I hope you are not thinking about leaving? Your shift has not finished yet.

Val

You know what you can do with your shift.

Annie brings Val her coat and Jenny with her four children all follow Val outside into a taxi. Twenty minutes later they arrive at number eleven Trinstead Road. Getting out of the taxi, they all face the house.

Jenny

Who lives here?

Val

You do.

The Truth at Last

Characters

Charlie

A Scottish man in his thirties, he is not only a manager in hospitality, but he is the love child of Celia and Val's husband, Ken.

Setting

The County Park

The Happy Convenience

The Manor House

The Truth at Last

Val is eating her breakfast as Carol comes rushing down the stairs.

Carol
I'm going to be late.

Val
You have not been there five minutes and you're already starting to be late.

Carol
It's not my fault a certain person wanted to buy me one for the road.

Val
You could have always said no.

Carol
I could, but it was a double vodka.

Val
All I can say is I hope he is worth it.

Carol
I think so.

Val
The bus is due in five minutes; you'd better get running down that street.

Carol
I'll see you later. *(Giving Val a hug)*

Carol rushes out of the door and is seen running down the street. Ten minutes later, there is a knock on Val's door. Val goes to open it.

Val
Don't tell me you have missed the bus.

Tony
I hope not.

Val
Hello, I've not seen you for ages. Are you sure you're at the right door?

Tony

I know I'm at the right door.

Val

Are those flowers for me?

Tony

They are. They are to say sorry for the way I've behaved. Judy's just told me why you couldn't go on our date the other week.

Val

And if you had not stormed off, I would have told you why.

Tony

I know. It was just that I had been so looking forward to spending time with you.

Val

Let's spend time together now. Do you fancy a walk, there is something I need to do.

Tony

That sounds good.

Val goes inside to put her coat on. Five minutes later she appears at the door, holding a bag.

Val

Shall we go?

Tony

Yes.

Both Val and Tony walk up the road arm in arm, cutting through the estate they come out onto a country lane. Walking to the top of the lane they turn right and ascend a small hill.

Val

Have you been this way before?

Tony

I haven't

Val

Then I'll be your tour guide.

Tony

I'm all ears.

Val

If you look to your left you will see the lodge. It was built around 1840 for the Dukes of St Albanes, they were descendants of Nell Gwyn who as I'm sure you know was one of the mistresses of Charles II. it is said he had a hunting lodge on this very site.

Tony

Interesting.

They take a right at the top of the hill which leads to a dirt track. After a ten minutes' walk, they can see Alexander Lodges.

Val

Here we have Alexandra Lodges which was the main entrance to the lodge. They were built at the same time as the lodge.

Tony

You can imagine carriages coming this way up to the big house. Which way now?

Val

We turn right.

They both walk over the old quarry, which is now a nature reserve, until they reach an old oak tree which is standing on a mount overlooking the quarry and the surrounding countryside.

Tony

It might be a freezing cold day, but this long walk has certainly warmed me up.

Val

Now, I bet you are wondering why I have brought you to this tree when there are so many trees nearer to home?

Tony

It had crossed my mind.

Val

Two dear old people who had been married for over seventy years, died not so long ago. This tree is where they had their first kiss, and because of that they asked me to bury their ashes under it.

Tony

That is so romantic.

Val

It is. *(Taking a small trowel out of her bag)* could you do the honours please?

Tony

Go on then. *(Digging)* The ground is a bit hard.

Val

Well, we have been having some frosts.

After ten minutes, the hole is dug and Val, taking each of the containers with their ashes in, puts them in the hole side by side. She then covers them up and places a small wooden cross into the ground.

Tony

Nicely done.

Val

(Looking at the tree) I hope they are both enjoying their next adventure.

Tony

Let's hope it is together.

Val

Those two will never be separated, not even in death.

Tony

Did you say they had their first kiss here and were in love for the next seventy years?

Val

I did.

Tony

(Stealing a quick kiss) Now we have got seventy years of togetherness.

Val

It looks like it.

They both stand under the tree, lips embracing each other.

Tony

I have wanted to do that for a very long time.

Val

Me too, although there is something I should tell you.

Tony

That sounds worrying.

Val

I am leaving to live abroad.

Tony

And I've only just found you. Where are you going?

Val

I'm spending the first six months in Spain and then, who knows where I'll be in the world.

Tony

It could be lonely on your own.

Val

Who's to say I will be on my own?

Tony

They say love never runs smoothly.

Val

Well, I've told you my plans, I'm leaving on Boxing Day. The flight and accommodation are all booked, but I'm not pressuring you, you must make up your mind on your own.

Tony

I do need time to think. I'm spending a few weeks in Devon with my daughter, she has some issues and she needs my support at this time.

Val

That is fine. You take as long as you need.

They both walk back, arm in arm until the reach Val's gate.

Tony

Thank you for a lovely morning.

Val

You are very welcome. I must dash or I will be late for work again. You have a great day.

Tony
>You too.

Val goes inside and gets ready for work. After feeding the cat who has started to come into the house, Val catches the Bus and after twenty minutes she walks to the main entrance of the Happy Convenience.

Karen
>*(Shouting)* Val, have you got a minute?

Val
>Not really, but I'm late anyway.

Val walks over to the foodbank.

Karen
>I just thought I would give you an update.

Val
>What's been happening?

Karen
>Jamie.

Val
>So you have seen him then?

Karen
>He came to the foodbank the other week. He wasn't the easiest person to talk to, but I got Billy to persuade him to talk to his mother and she said he had too many issues to go back to the streets, so she has moved him in with her. He is now her lodger.

Val
>Who would of thought, a few weeks ago she was on the 'game' and going nowhere in life. Now she is a woman who is so driven and caring, we should be calling her saint Sharon. What does Billy think of the new lodger?

Karen
>Billy is not living there now.

Val
>Where is he living?

Karen
>With me.

Val

Is he. You're old enough to understand what you are doing. Just be careful and make sure he is the one before you start having a family.

Karen

I will.

Val

While I think about it,

Karen

Yes?

Val

Firstly, what do you think to having Christmas Day at the foodbank? We can invite all those families who wouldn't be able to afford a Christmas dinner.

Karen

What a good idea. We could decorate the place and even have Santa come and give out presents.

Val

A super idea.

Karen

Was there something else you wanted to ask?

Val

Are you doing anything tonight?

Karen

I was going to put my feet up and watch a film on the tele.

Val

That's what you thought you were going to do.

Karen

Am I not?

Val

No, you are my plus one at Celia's engagement party.

Karen

Really?

Val

Really. Be at mine for seven.

Karen

Do I have to?

Val

Yes, see you later.

Val leaves the foodbank and walks to the main entrance of The Happy Convenience. As she walks through the door, Sarah is standing there looking cross.

Sarah

Can you follow me to my office Mrs Johnson.

Val

Of course.

They both walk to Sarah's office.

Sarah

(Sitting down) Once again Mrs Johnson, you are late. This now seems to be happening on a regular basis. It's bad enough that you left halfway through your shift the other week, but then to keep on being late, this cannot carry on. I have no choice but to give you a written warning. *(Sarah passes Val her written warning)*

Val

Thank you Miss Viola.

Sarah

You are lucky it's not a letter of dismissal. Have you got anything to say?

Val

Do you know Miss Viola, in a strange way I'm going to miss you. I can only thank you for educating me in how not to treat people. I don't think I could have helped so many without your abilities to show a disregard of human suffering. Just as you have given me my written warning, I now give you my resignation letter. I'll be knocking on your door for my P45 very soon.

Sarah

(Looking shocked) I'm sure some people will miss you. I want you to start on clothes and then move to the tills. As you are

leaving, there is no point in keeping you in one place. You can go now, I'm far too busy to talk anymore. After all, we are now in our busiest period.

Val walks out of Sarah's office with a smile on her face. In the next six hours, Val finds herself working all over the supermarket, which she enjoyed as she gets to work with many of her friends, possibly for the last time. At five o'clock, Val gets onto the bus.

Frank

Good afternoon young lady.

Val

Good afternoon young man.

Frank

It's a good job we both have good manners.

Val

Isn't it just. Which reminds me, I need to ask you a favour if it is possible?

Frank

If it's you that is doing the asking, then anything is possible. Sit yourself down there and tell me as I'm driving.

Val

(Sitting down) As you know, Christmas is coming up.

Frank

It is. When we were at school Christmas seemed like every two years.

Val

That's true. Now it seems like it's every six months.

Frank

Very true.

Val

Anyway, on Christmas Day we are going to give all the families a Christmas dinner at the food bank for those who can't afford it.

Frank

What a nice idea.

Val

Now as you know as well as me, no buses run on Christmas Day and a taxi would cost you an arm and a leg. So what I was thinking.

Frank

Yes?

Val

If it is possible,

Frank

Spit it out woman.

Val

Could you borrow a bus and pick up anyone who would like a Christmas dinner?

Frank

And who is going to drive this bus on Christmas Day?

Val

Someone kind-hearted and who thinks of others.

Frank

I don't know who that could be. *(Smiling)* Leave it with me, I'll have a word with Santa.

Frank stops the bus outside Val's house.

Val

Thank you Frank. You would make a wonderful Santa.

Frank

HO HO HO.

Getting off the bus, Val rushes into the house

Val

Carol is the immersion heater on?

Carol

It's been on for the last hour.

Val rushes upstairs and heads straight for the bathroom. An hour later Val descends the stairs wearing a black cocktail dress with a pink jacket.

Val

Pour us a large one Carol love.

Carol

Well look at you. You look wonderful.

Val

Thanks love. Now while I've got you, I need to tell you something.

Carol

You're not throwing me out?

Val

Far from it. I'm the one who's leaving.

Carol

You're not?

Val

I'm catching a flight to Spain on Boxing Day.

Carol

How long for?

Val

I've booked an apartment for six months, and then who knows where I'll be. Don't worry, I'm not leaving you with all the bills. The gas and electricity I have paid up until the summer so all you will need is your food and the phone. I expect you to look after the place, and if you have any problems go and see Lillian or Molly and don't forget to feed the cat, although by the looks of it he has already moved in. *(The cat is sitting on the sofa)* Don't worry, you will be fine, and this new bloke you have got, please don't rush into anything, you know what happened last time.

Carol

I won't.

Val

And Carol...

Carol

What?

Val

The bills are your responsibility, not any mans.

Carol

I'll take care of them.

Val

Right, that's my taxi, I'll see you later.

Val rushes outside and into the taxi.

Karen

I can't believe I'm going to Celia's engagement party.

Val

With her love life, I bet she can't believe it either. *(They both laugh)*

Karen

Now, I've heard a rumour. Two in fact.

Val

Those jungle drums never stop.

Karen

Spain, is it?

Val

It is. For six months and then who knows.

Karen

So, what's brought this on?

Val

My age and a willingness to travel. Do you know I've been to four funerals this year, the first one being my husband. None of those people got the chance to travel. It's a beautiful world and I want to see more of it.

Karen

So really death has persuaded you.

Val

It has. You never know what is around the corner.

Karen

True. It will be a bus in my case. *(They both laugh)* Whose this man Tony?

Val

He was at Judy's party; did you not see him?

Karen

I can't remember him.

Val

No, you wouldn't. You had other things on your mind that night didn't you slut. *(They both laugh)*

Karen

So, is he going with you?

Val

No idea. He has gone down to Devon to see his daughter, I've heard nothing.

Karen

He'll be a fool not to go with you.

Val

He knows when I'm going and where I'm going. There is nothing more I can do.

The taxi pulls up outside the Manor House.

Karen

Wow, how big is this place?

Val

I hear they only cater for the wealthy.

Karen

Should we be here?

Val

We are as good as anyone else, so why not.

They both get out of the taxi and walk up the long drive to the main entrance. Seeing that the door is open, they both walk in.

Karen

I can hear music, so that must be us.

They both walk along a small corridor until they come to another set of doors. Opening the doors, they walk into a large room which has been decorated with an engagement theme in mind. At the side of the room is a pianist and on the back wall is all the foods you would love to try but could never afford. The bar is situated in an adjoining room. Celia walks over.

Celia

Val my love, how are you? *(They embrace)*

Val

I'm good. What a beautiful house, and the food looks amazing.

Celia

Isn't it. The house was built for Lord Summers and has been visited by many royals over its four hundred years. We only managed to book this place because the manager is a friend of my future husband.

Val

It's so good to have friends with benefits. *(Mr Scott walks over)*

Mr Scott

Mrs Johnson, it's so nice of you to come.

Val

It's my pleasure.

Mr Scott

I've heard you are leaving us soon?

Val

I am. It's time for me to see some of the world before it's too late.

Mr Scott

Good for you, and send me the bill for the Christmas dinners, it can be my present to the estate.

Val

You are so kind.

Mr Scott

I see you and Miss Millar have not got a drink yet. Let me get the manager for you. Charlie!

Charlie

Yes Mr Scott.

Mr Scott

Could you escort Mrs Johnson and Miss Miller to the bar. It's a free bar so order anything you want.

Val
Thank you.

Charlie
Ladies, would you like to follow me. *(All three of them walk to the bar)* Louise *(The barmaid)* give these ladies whatever they want.

Louise
Yes of course.

Val
(To Charlie) You have a familiar face, have we met before?

Charlie
Not as I can recall. As you can tell by my accent, I was born and lived in Scotland for many years.

Val
Is your mother still alive?

Charlie
She is, but I was brought up by my great aunt.

Val
Is your father still alive?

Charlie
No. He died about a year ago, but he did come and see me from time to time as I was growing up.

Val
Interesting. Have you got your own family now?

Charlie
Two girls and a boy.

Val
I bet they are delightful.

Charlie
They are.

Val
It must be nice to have such good friends like Mr Scott.

Charlie
Mr Scott?

Val
Is he not a good friend?

Charlie
It's the first time I've met him. It is Miss La-One who is a friend. Would you excuse me. *(He walks off)*

Val and Karen get their drinks and go to the buffet.

Karen
Did you see that snooty bitch Celia, she never even spoke to me once.

Val
You couldn't buy that luck. But this amazing food is speaking to us. Tuck in.

Karen
I bet you couldn't buy this food in The Happy Convenience.

Val
You can't. Nobody could afford it.

Both Val and Karen sit down next to the pianist.

Karen
How the other half live.

Val
No wonder there were revolutions in countries like France and Russia. If you are going to have a capitalist system, then there is always going to be those at the top and those at the bottom.

Charlie walks by Val's table

Karen
Something is bothering you?

Val
You see that guy who has just walked by our table?

Karen
Yes?

Val

His face is familiar, but I just can't think where I've seen it.

Karen

This food is good.

Val

Go ahead and get yourself some more.

Karen

But they'll think I'm being greedy.

Val

Sod them, on your way to the buffet get me another drink, it's free.

Karen goes off to the bar while Val is staring at Charlie, thinking where she has seen his face before. Celia walks past Val's table.

Celia

It's a shame Ken is not with us anymore; he would have loved this. I'm off to the loo. *(Celia walks towards the toilets)*

All of a sudden Val remembers where she has seen Charlie's face before and rushes over to Charlie.

Val

Can you tell me how often you saw your father?

Charlie

Probably three or four times in the winter months, but in the summer months I would see him three or four times a month.

Val

What job did he do?

Charlie

He was a coach driver. He did tours around Scotland.

Rushing off, Val heads towards the toilets. As she opens the door, she sees Celia washing her hands.

Val

You vile, cheating bitch.

Celia

Are you talking to me?

Val

Too right I am. Why, of all the blokes you could have had, you had to choose my husband.

Celia

I don't know what you're talking about?

Val

I bet you don't. You lying cow. Charlie is yours and Ken's son. Isn't he. I bet Charlie is thirty years of age, because it was thirty years ago that you decided to have a year off and go travelling. You got as far as Scotland didn't you. Who was the woman you left your child with?

Celia

My aunt. She couldn't have any children of her own.

Val

Now things make sense. The reason why he kept on driving the coaches when he could have got more money doing the buses. The reason why he was always doing overtime, with some nights he didn't get home till gone twelve and I thought it was the over time that was making him so tired, but it was banging you every night wasn't it? That's why he fell asleep when our daughter was taking her last breath. I bet he had his heart attack while you were on top of him. What had I ever done to you?

Celia

Nothing.

Val

So why?

Celia

Love.

Val

Hence the reason why you collapsed at his grave. I should tell everyone what you have done, but then I would be just as vile as you. You have to live the rest of your miserable life knowing what you did to me and my daughter. Don't ever speak to me again. You don't exist.

Val opens the toilet door and walks out with her head held high.

It's Time to Go

Setting
Val's house and garden

The number 64 bus

The Happy Convenience

The foodbank

Spanish apartment

It's Time to Go

It is Christmas Eve and Carol is putting the Christmas tree up. Val walks down the stairs.

Val

That tree brings back a lot of memories.

Carol

If they are too painful, I'll take it down.

Val

Don't be silly. But do me a favour, you will find a Fairy who has a violin. Make sure you put her at the top of the tree. I used to tell my beautiful daughter that when we are all in bed, she plays her violin as Santa is on his way. Also, don't forget to leave a glass of sherry and a mince pie for Santa.

Carol

Really?

Val

Yes. George the cat is expecting a lot of presents this year. *(They both laugh)*

Carol

Don't you just love traditions at Christmas. Every family have them.

Val

What shift you on?

Carol

I'm not on till the day after Boxing Day.

Val

Lucky you.

Carol

What time are you on today?

Val

Ten till two.

Carol

Your last shift.

Val

It is. But all good things must come to an end.

Carol

I bet you are feeling a bit sad?

Val

I am. To say goodbye to people you have worked with for twenty years is always sad. But I'm also excited to see where life is going to take me next. Sometimes you have to take a leap of faith. Right, I'd better go, the bus is due.

Carol

I'll see you later.

Val

And Carol?

Carol

What?

Val

Does the cat really need to be decorated too? *(They both laugh)*

Val makes her way to the bus stop for the last time. As Val walks by each of the houses she reflects on all the different people who have lived in them over the years. People who would never have let their gardens become the jungles they are now. Where once doors were open to help and advise, they were now firmly shut. Bev is standing at her door.

Bev

Hello Val.

Val

Hello.

Bev

I hear you have got Carol staying at yours?

Val

I have. She is doing so well. She has got herself a job and a new man in her life. I've heard they have laid you off, and I was shocked to hear that your husband was playing away. Merry Christmas to you.

The bus comes down the hill and stops at the bus stop. Opening the door, Val sees that Frank is the driver.

Frank

Here comes Santa's little helper.

Val

Morning Frank. Are we all set for tomorrow?

Frank

Everything is under control. Put your money away and go sit down. It's Christmas.

Val

Thank you Frank.

Val sits down behind Mrs Irons.

Mrs Irons

Merry Christmas Val.

Val

I don't know if it's appropriate seeing that your husband passed away only a month ago, but happy Christmas to you too.

Mrs Irons

We all must go one day, and life is too short for grieving. That's why like you, this is my last day at work. You have inspired me to get out there and seek new adventures.

Val

Good for you. What are you doing tomorrow?

Mrs Irons

Not a lot. Theres not much point in cooking a Christmas dinner for one.

Val

Frank?

Frank

What?

Val

Don't forget to pick up Mrs Irons tomorrow.

Frank

I won't.

Val

There has been a lot of changes over the years on this estate and there is very few of the old ones left. But those few who are would never leave someone on their own at Christmas.

Mrs Irons

Thank you.

Frank stops at the next stop. Vicky, Violet, Tom, and Brian get onto the bus. They all say good morning to both Val and Mrs Irons. Two stops down Ricky and his boyfriend Gary gets on the bus.

Ricky

Good morning everyone. *(They all say good morning)*

The next stop down, Deb and Rose get on the bus, followed by Pam and Annie.

Val

Bloody hell, it seems the whole estate is on the bus this morning.

At the next stop Judy gets on the bus with two bunches of flowers. Frank turns his engine off.

Mrs Irons

Are we being kidnapped?

Frank

No Mrs Irons, you and Val are being awarded the bus passenger lifetime achievement award.

Mrs Irons

That's wonderful.

Judy

Mrs Irons, for over seventy years you have been a permanent fixture on the number 64 bus. We will all miss your frankness and honesty which at times is shocking, but you have always stuck to the belief that honesty is the best policy. A round of applause for Mrs Irons.

Mrs Irons gets out of her seat and collects her flowers.

Mrs Irons

Thank you so much everyone. I hope someone else enjoys the

number 64 bus as much as I have over the years. Thank you from the bottom of my heart.

Judy

Have a wonderful retirement. *(Everyone claps and cheers)*

Val

Is it my turn now?

Judy

It definitely is. A friend and inspiration to so many. You are not only going to be missed on this bus, but on the estate and in The Happy Convenience as well. They don't make them like Val anymore. Thank you for being there for some many and for so long. Whatever bus you get on in the world, think of the wonderful times you had with your friends. Our Val everyone!

Val gets up out of her seat and goes to the front of the bus to collect her award and her bunch of flowers.

Val

It's not only been a privilege and an honour being a passenger on this bus, but an honour and a privilege to have lived on an estate side by side with some amazing people. I'm working class and I'm proud of it. *(Everyone claps)* Thank you everyone, and Merry Christmas to you all.

Everyone shouts out Merry Christmas as they clap and cheer.

Frank

Right, I'd better get you lot to work. *(He starts up the engine)*

Five minutes later, Frank stops outside The Happy Convenience. As they all start to get off the bus, they hug and say goodbye to Mrs Irons and wish Frank a Merry Christmas. Val, Judy, Deb, Rose, Pam and Annie all walk towards The Happy Convenience arm in arm. When they get to the entrance, Sarah Viola is waiting.

Val

I'll put money on that she is waiting for me, I'll see you later ladies.

Sarah

Mrs Johnson, can you follow me to my office.

Val

Certainly.

Val follows Sarah to her office where they both sit down.

Sarah

Now, as this is your last day, I must formally give you your p45.

Val

Thank you, but I'm not planning on using it again. But life sometimes plays nasty tricks on you, and you're forced back into the job market.

Sarah

That's very true. Now the formal part is over, I want to take this opportunity to not only thank you for your many years of service, but on a personal note, thank you for saving my life.

Val

Think nothing of it. I did what anyone else would have done.

Sarah

In saving my life, I doubt it. I do have a surprise for you later. You are on till number one.

Val walks out of Sarah's office and five minutes later is sitting ready for her first customer.

Shelley

You should get off with a quiet last shift. I think most people have done their shopping by now. Although like me there is always something you forget.

Shelley puts a tin of Quality Street onto the conveyor belt. Val scans it.

Val

That will be five pounds fifty please,

Shelley

(Gives Val the money) Thank you.

Val

Who is the lucky person to receive chocolates on Christmas eve?

Shelley

You are. Merry Christmas Val.

Val

Shelley, you are a star. *(They both hug)*

Just as they are hugging, there is a message over the loudspeaker.

'We would just like to inform everyone that it is Val Johnsons last day with us. So, if anyone would like to say goodbye, you will find her on till number one. Happy Christmas everyone!'

Ten minutes later Val has a queue a mile long with the flower's section all sold out. It takes over an hour for everyone in the queue to say their goodbyes.

Val

(To Shelley) So much for a quiet shift. Is it time for me to go home yet?

Shelley

Another half an hour and you will have made it.

Another announcement is made on the loudspeaker.

'Can all staff go to till number one please.'

Val

What is going on now?

All the staff gather and Sarah Viola walks over and stands by the conveyor belt.

Sarah

Today one of our family is leaving us to travel the world. I'm sure there are many of us that wish we could fit into her suitcase. *(They all laugh)* We all wish you an amazing time and who knows, you might even give us a thought as you're travelling around the world. *(Everyone laughs)* But we all wish you well. *(Everyone claps)* I have just one more thing to do then I'll let you go, I promise. Now, we all know that not only has Val been amazing at The Happy Convenience but also on the estate that she has called home for many years. Val has helped and cared for so many on this estate and although she is leaving us, her idea to set up the foodbank which helps so many people on a daily basis means that

Val's caring and kindness will continue for many years to come. And on a personal note, if it wasn't for Val, three adults and a child wouldn't be standing here today. Because of this, a few days ago I received a letter, which is in my hand, from Buckingham Palace. Saying that Mrs Valerie Johnson has been awarded the OBE for her bravery and service to her community. *(Everyone cheers)*

Val

(With tears in her eyes) I thank you all so much from the bottom of my heart. It's been a privilege and an honour to work and live with so many wonderful people. If I had the chance to do it all again, I would do it in a heartbeat. As for my OBE who would have thought a working-class girl who has lived on an estate nearly all her life, is going to Buckingham Palace, you couldn't make it up. Thank you everyone, and Merry Christmas to you all. *(Everyone claps)*

Shelley

The taxi is here. We have put all your presents in the taxi so let's be having you Mrs Johnson.

Putting her coat on, Val walks to the main entrance where everyone is standing. Giving Sarah a big hug Val walks out of the door and before she gets into the taxi, she takes one final look at The Happy Convenience and at the people who work there. Getting unto the taxi, everyone waves her off. The next morning Val walks down the stairs to see a Christmas breakfast laid out on the table.

Carol

Merry Christmas Val.

Val

Merry Christmas Carol, you shouldn't have gone to all this trouble.

Carol

You are worth it.

Val

It looks delicious and wine for breakfast? It must be Christmas day.

Carol

(Looking under the Christmas tree) I can see Santa has been.

Val

We must have been good girls this year.

Carol

You certainly have.

Val

(Finishing her breakfast) Lets see what he has brought you.

Carol

These can't all be for me?

Val

Where you have been they certainly are.

Carol opens all her presents and gives Val a hug after each one.

Carol

Val you are so kind.

Val

Don't be silly now I have one more for you.

Carol

You have brought me enough.

Val

I thought it was time for you to start wearing your own clothes and not my second-hand stuff.

Carol

A two-hundred-pound voucher? Val, you shouldn't have.

Val

Every woman needs their own clothes to wear.

Carol

Thank you Val. Look, there are two presents under the tree.

George the cat walks into the living room and sits under the tree.

Val

By the looks of it, he's hoping one of those presents is his.

Carol

George, shall we have a look. *(George purrs)* Look George, this one has got your name on. *(As Carols opens it, George starts to play with one of his toys)*

Val

Well, he's a happy cat. Things we buy and say to our pets. Is that all the presents gone?

Carol

Not quite. There is one left.

Val

I don't know who's that one is for?

Carol

Let me have a look. It says, 'To Val, Merry Christmas.'

Val

Carol you've not?

Carol

It's from Santa, here, open it.

Val

(Opening her present) Carol, it's beautiful.

Carol

I thought it you had a cross on your neck, God will protect you on your travels.

Val

I will always wear it. Come here and give me a hug. *(After five minutes, they let go)*

Carol

What time's the bus coming?

Val

If it's on time it should be here at twelve. That gives me enough time to go and see the gossip girls.

Carol

Good luck with that.

Val puts three wine glasses and a bottle of wine onto a tray. She walks next door to the late Mrs Edwards Garden. Finding a crate, Val stands on it and looks over the wall, she puts the tray on the top of the wall.

Val

Lillian, are you there?

Lillian

Is it snowing?

Val

It is, get your washing in.

Lillian

(Comes charging out with her clothes basket) I've not got any washing out, what am I like.

Val

I know what you would like.

Lillian

What?

Val

A glass of wine?

Lillian

(Standing on a box) I shouldn't be doing this at this time in the morning, but it is Christmas Day. Molly are you there?

Molly

(Running out) Don't tell me someone's got their washing out on Christmas Day?

Val

No, but we have got a glass of wine out.

Molly

Alcohol at this time of the morning? Shocking.

Lillian

So, you don't want any then?

Molly

Well, it is Christmas.

Molly comes round to Lillian's Garden and stand on a crate looking over the wall.

Val

Ladies, Merry Christmas.

Lillian/Molly

Merry Christmas. *(As they raise their glasses)*

Val

We have had some good times chatting over these walls.

Lillian

Haven't we just.

Molly

It would have been so nice if four of us were standing here and not three.

Val

She was a very special lady.

Lillian

She was.

Molly

It wasn't long before the for-sale sign went up?

Lillian

She could have only been dead a few weeks - that vile man.

Val

If someone's going to be making money them principles soon go out of the window.

Molly

Let's hope that the new owner does everything the working-class way.

Val

What way is that then?

Molly

Doing the jobs on the right days and at the right times. If they do not put their washing out on a Monday then we will know if they are good neighbours or not.

Val

Are you going to your daughters for dinner?

Lillian

I am, but I don't mind telling you, her husband makes me feel uncomfortable.

Val

Why's that?

Lillian

He doesn't drink alcohol.

Molly

He doesn't what?

Lillian

He doesn't drink alcohol.

Molly

You mean to say a working-class bloke who lives on a council estate, doesn't drink alcohol.

Lillian

That's right.

Molly

He needs to go and see the doctor.

Lillian

He doesn't smoke either.

Molly

No wonder you feel uncomfortable. That would put me right off my food.

Val

Are you off to your Robert's?

Molly

Yes. He will have had forty fags and be half pissed as we sit down to eat. Now that is a proper Christmas.

Val

Ladies, I've got to go. Now you will keep an eye on Carol, won't you?

Lillian

Don't you worry, she will be fine with us.

Molly

We will make sure she does the house jobs on the right days, and if her new bloke moves in, we'll make sure if he is washing his car or doing the garden, it will only be on the weekends.

Val
You are both stars. Merry Christmas to you both.

Lillian
(Giving Val a hug) Merry Christmas and have a wonderful time.

Molly
Merry Christmas to you my darling. We will be thinking of you. *(She gives Val a hug)*

Back in the house Val realises the time.

Val
Carol, the bus will be here in a minute.

Carol
Don't worry, I've got your coat and scarf.

They both head out and stand by the gate. Two minutes later they can hear jingle bells as the bus pulls up.

Val
Wow Frank this looks amazing.

Carol
It's like Santa's Grotto.

Frank
It's looking good if I say so myself. Now the presents are over there with the names on the children's presents. Right, hold on ladies, here we go! Ho ho ho go!

At the next stop Jenny and her four children get on the bus.

Val
Merry Christmas Jenny.

Jenny
Merry Christmas. Although I couldn't afford to buy much for the children.

Val
That's not a problem, have you seen all those presents stacked up over there.

Jenny
Yes.

Val
> They are all for you and the kids.

Jenny
> Val...

Val
> No tears, its Christmas. *(They hug)* Frank, onto the next stop.

At the next stop is Sharon and Jamie.

Sharon
> Merry Christmas.

Val
> Merry Christmas. You are that shining star we all follow.

Sharon
> Stop it.

Val
> Merry Christmas Jamie.

Jamie
> Merry Christmas Mrs Johnson.

Val
> *(Opening her arms)* It is Christmas.

Jamie walks into Val's arms with tears in his eyes.

Jamie
> Thank you.

Val
> Sharon?

Sharon
> What?

Val
> Is Jamie off to college next year?

Sharon
> He certainly is. And two years later he will be at university.

Val
> *(With Jamie still in her arms)* Don't let your past rule your future. You are going to be an amazing success. Now go and see

what Santa has brought you.

Jamie
(Looking into Val's eyes) Thank you.

Val
Right Santa off to the next stop.

At the next stop Sophie and her children James and Lucy gets on the bus.

Sophie
Merry Christmas Val, everyone.

Everyone shouts Merry Christmas.

Val
(To the children) Hello there you two.

James/Lucy
Merry Christmas Aunty Val.

Val
Go and see what Santa has brought you.

Lucy
(Opening her present) New shoes!

Val
Right Frank, whenever you are ready.

For the next half an hour the bus makes numerous stops on its way to the food bank. At the food bank, frank opens his doors, and everyone rushes out and runs over to the food bank. As they rush inside, they can see it has been decorated with Christmas trees, balloons, and streamers. On the table everyone has got a name place card. Karen greets Val at the door with a big hug.

Karen
We did it.

Val
You mean you did. It looks wonderful, let's hope you can do this every year.

Karen
I hope so.

Val

(Giving Karen a present) A little something to say thank you.

Karen

You shouldn't have.

Val

Merry Christmas.

Karen

Merry Christmas Val.

Val

(Raising her glass) Merry Christmas everyone!

Everyone raises their glasses and shouts Merry Christmas.

Two months later the Spanish postman puts two letters through Val's door. Picking up the letters, Val goes to sit on her balcony with a glass of sangria. Sitting down, Val reads her first letter.

My dearest Val,

I thought I would just write you an update. The foodbank is going from strength to strength. With an increase of donations, we can help far more people now. Sharon is a godsend, the amount of people she has helped is amazing and Jamie has now started college and he seems very determined to succeed now. Mrs Edwards' old house has been sold and the new owners moved in a week ago. Although you would have thought World War Three had started when the new neighbours put some washing out on a Sunday. Carol has now moved her bloke in, and Molly is making sure he is washing his car and doing the garden only at the weekends. As for the cat, he now rules the house. Even on a night out Carol makes sure she is home early to feed the cat. The Happy Convenience is much the same. Although Sarah Viola is now dating a woman younger than herself. Who would have thought it. Hopefully in a couple of months I will come out and see you for a week.

Take care.
Love
Karen xx

Val reads her second letter.

Dear Val,

I've made it. I arrived a couple of weeks ago. Val, Africa is everything I wished it was. At the moment I'm in Kenya helping out at the local school and getting myself involved with wildlife projects. Val, to see animals like elephants, rhinos, and lions in the wild is just incredible. You must come out out see for yourself the wonders Africa has got to offer and like my mother, I've started dating a doctor, it seems history is repeating itself. I've left you my address. I hope to see you very soon.
Much love,
Poppy.

Val
> Tony.

Tony
> What?

Val
> Africa is our next adventure.

Tony
> I can't wait.

Printed in Great Britain
by Amazon

36500517R00129